Battle of Br

Hawker Hurricanes of No 238 Squadron at their base at Middle Wallop. Aircraft 'VK:G,' in the middle-ground, took part in the fighting on 15 September and was damaged in action that day. It was later repaired.

Spitfires of No 41 Squadron during the Battle. The further aircraft, 'EB:K,' was lost in action on 15 October.

Battle of Britain

Alfred Price

DAILY EXPRESS
ARMS AND
ARMOUR PRESS

First published in Great Britain in 1990 by Arms and Armour Press, Artillery House, Artillery Row, London SW1P 1RT. for Express Newspapers PLC

Designed and edited by DAG Publications Ltd. Designed by David Gibbons; edited by David Dorrell; layout by David Gibbons; diagrams by Cilla Eurich; typeset by Typesetters (Birmingham) Ltd, Warley; camerawork by M&E Reproductions, North Fambridge, Essex; printed and bound in Yugoslavia.

◄Overleaf: 'FREEMA SQUADRON, SCRAMBLE!'

KENLEY, 12.55 PM, 18 AUGUST. Squadron Leader Donald MacDonell leads a scramble take-off of eight Spitfires of No 64 Squadron. MacDonell described the process of scrambling a squadron during the Battle of Britain in these words:

'The Orderly answering the telephone would shout "Scramble!" at the top of his voice and each pilot would dash for his aircraft. By the time I reached my Spitfire the mechanic would have started the engine. He got out of the cockpit and I got in, and he helped me strap into my parachute. Then he passed the seat straps and helped me fasten them. When I gave the thumbs up he would shut the side door, jump to the ground and run round in front of the port wing. Meanwhile I tightened my various straps, pulled on my helmet and plugged in the R/T lead. After checking that the engine was running properly, I would wave the groundcrew to pull away the chocks, open the throttle, and move forward out of my blast pen.

'After a fast taxi across the grass to the take-off position I would line up, open the throttle wide and begin my take-off run. The rest of my pilots followed me as fast as they could. The whole thing, from the scramble order to the last aircraft leaving the ground, took about a minute and a half.

'As soon as we were off the ground and climbing, I would inform operations "Freema Squadron airborne" [Freema was No 64 Squadron's radio call-sign]. The Sector Controller would come back and tell me where he wanted me to go and at what altitude. While the squadron was forming up I would climb in a wide spiral at low boost, until everyone was in place. Then I would open up to a high throttle setting to get to altitude as fast as possible.'

When his squadron was airborne and formed up, MacDonell received orders to patrol over base at 20,000 feet. The unit would be in position and ready to engage when, twenty-five minutes later, a large formation of Dorniers with fighter escort ran in to bomb Kenley from high altitude.

The painting shows the scene at Kenley as MacDonell led his squadron into the air and the ground staff were preparing for a possible enemy attack. The Spitfire in the foreground is unserviceable and is being pushed to a place of relative safety at the side of the airfield beside one of the revetments. The refuelling vehicle is being waved to a point beside the airfield boundary clear of all aircraft, where it will cause least damage if it is set on fire.

ACKNOWLEDGEMENTS

It would have been impossible to assemble the material for this book without the generous assistance of many people. I should like to thank the following eye-witnesses for allowing me to use their stories: Air Vice-Marshal Desmond Hughes, Air Commodore Donald MacDonell, Group Captain Dennis David, Wing Commander Innes Westmacott, Squadron Leader Harry Newton, Kenneth Lee, John Etherington, Michael Crossley, Elaine Lewis and Vera Saies who served with the Royal Air Force; and General Adolf Galland, General Roderich Cescotti, Colonel Julius Neumann, Heinz Kirsch, Max Gruber, Hans Schmoller-Haldy, Gerhard Schoepfel, Guenther Unger, Horst Schultz, Wilhelm Raab, Rolf Heitsch, Victor Kraft, Theodor Rehm and Horst Goetz who served in the Luftwaffe. Amelia Sopp, Peter Elstob, Alexander McKee and Walter Chesney described the actions as seen from the ground.

I am deeply grateful to Winston and Gordon Ramsey for making available to me some of the excellent photographs they had collected for their volumes on *The Blitz, Then and Now*. Thanks are also due to Hans Ring, Arno Abendroth, Dilip Sarkar, Alan White, Peter Cornwell, Andy Sanders, Sir Richard Pease, and Hanfried Schliephake who kindly let me use their photographs and other material.

I am grateful to John Batchelor for allowing me to use his superb colour artwork. Jim Mitchell, the artist who painted the action scenes, was a joy to work with and spared no effort to ensure that the events were shown as accurately as possible.

Alfred Price, Uppingham, Rutland.

Messerschmitt 110 of DG 26 (shot down by MacDonell following the scramble on 18 August) after it crash-landed near Lydd.

Contents

RAF FIGHTER COMMAND, 1940: GROUPS, SECTORS AND SQUADRONS

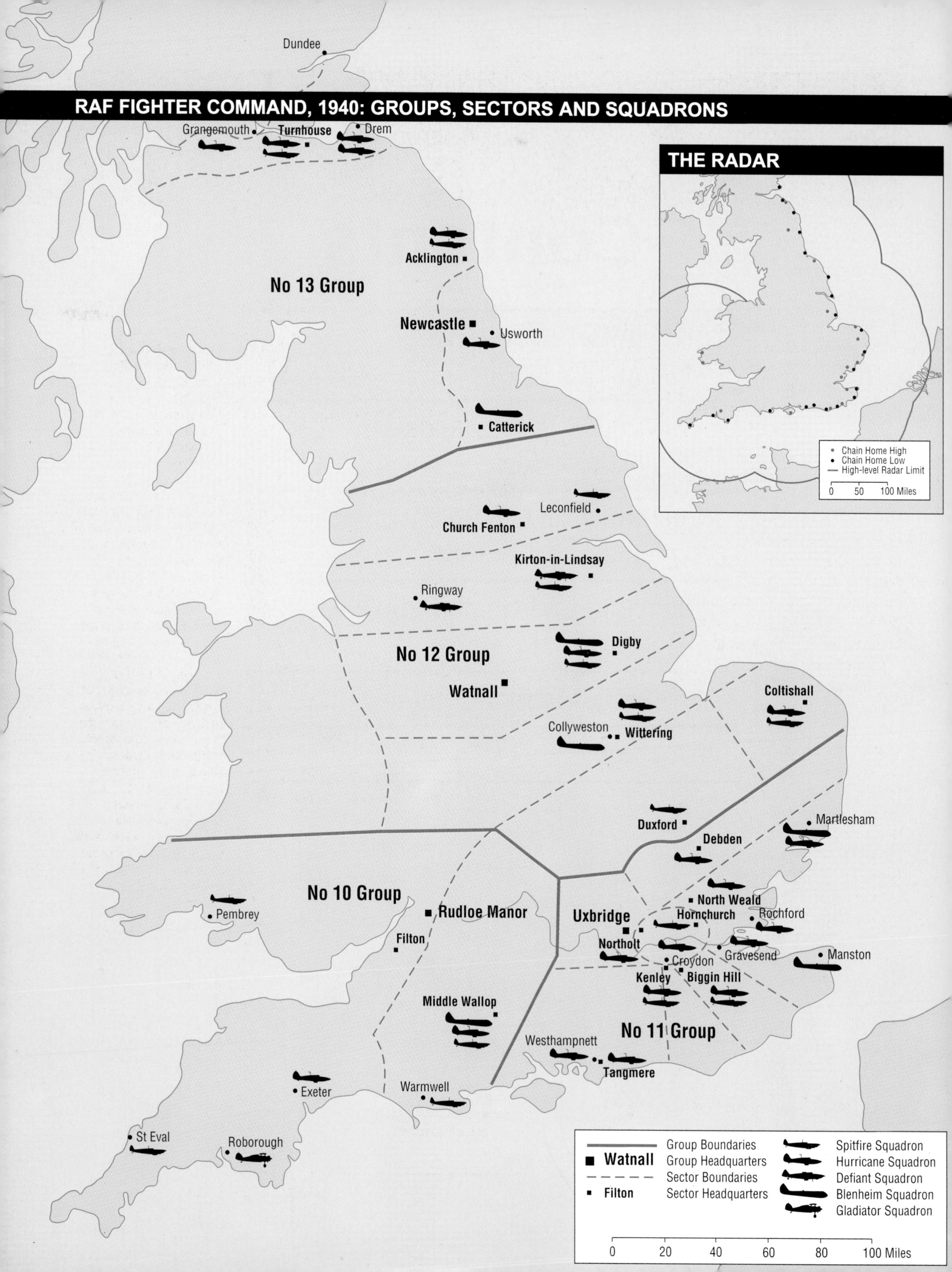

Dundee

Grangemouth • Turnhouse • Drem

No 13 Group

Acklington

Newcastle • Usworth

Catterick

Leconfield

Church Fenton

Kirton-in-Lindsay

Ringway

Digby

No 12 Group

Watnall

Coltishall

Collyweston • Wittering

Duxford

Martlesham

Debden

North Weald • Rochford

No 10 Group

Pembrey

Hornchurch

Rudloe Manor

Uxbridge

Northolt

Gravesend • Manston

Filton

Croydon

Kenley • Biggin Hill

Middle Wallop

Westhampnett

No 11 Group

Tangmere

Exeter

Warmwell

St Eval

Roborough

THE RADAR

• Chain Home High
• Chain Home Low
— High-level Radar Limit

0   50   100 Miles

▬	**Watnall**	Group Boundaries / Group Headquarters
– – –		Sector Boundaries
▪	**Filton**	Sector Headquarters

Spitfire Squadron
Hurricane Squadron
Defiant Squadron
Blenheim Squadron
Gladiator Squadron

0   20   40   60   80   100 Miles

1. THE INITIAL SKIRMISHES
10 July to 12 August

'What General Weygand called the "Battle of France" is over. I expect the "Battle of Britain" is about to begin.'
Winston Churchill speaking in the House of Commons, 18 June 1940

AT THE BEGINNING OF JULY 1940 the citizens of the British Isles faced a peril greater than at any time since the despatch of the Spanish Armada in 1588. Seven weeks earlier Adolf Hitler had launched his army in an overwhelmingly successful blitzkrieg campaign in the west that defeated the Dutch, the Belgian and then the French armies in quick succession. The British army in France had survived only by dint of a brilliantly improvised evacuation from the port of Dunkirk and the beaches to the east. Now the whole of the European coastline facing Britain, from North Cape in Norway to Biarritz in the south-west of France, was occupied by the German troops. Only Great Britain remained in the war and few Germans believed she could to hold out much longer.

Throughout June and the early part of July the German Government had launched several diplomatic initiatives inviting peace talks. With increasing impatience, Adolf Hitler waited for word that his sole remaining enemy accepted the reality of the situation – that continuing resistance was futile. If the British would see sense and make an early settlement, the German dictator reasoned, further bloodshed would be avoided and he could afford to be generous in his demands. But this course of reasoning showed no understanding of the nature of the new British Prime Minister, Winston Churchill. The Fuehrer waited in vain.

In a move calculated to bring increased pressure on the British Government, the German leader, early in July, ordered the Luftwaffe to prepare to launch a series of heavy attacks on targets in southern England. He informed his High Command:

'Since England, in spite of her hopeless military situation, shows no signs of being ready to come to an understanding, I have decided to prepare a landing operation against England and, if necessary, to carry it out.'

Air Chief Marshal Sir Hugh Dowding, 58, the Commander-in-Chief of Fighter Command during the Battle of Britain, bore the nickname 'Stuffy' and was regarded by his pilots as a cold aloof figure. Yet he was an exceptionally brilliant and far-sighted innovator, a 'technocrat' before the word had been invented. Dowding's previous post, between 1930 and 1936, had been that of Air Member for Research and Development on the Air Council. The period saw rapid technical changes and his department issued the specifications that led to the Spitfire, the Hurricane and other aircraft equipping the Royal Air Force during the Battle of Britain. Dowding had also pushed resources into the development of radar and integrated the new device into his system for controlling fighters. In the history of air warfare, no other commander played so large a part in the development of the equipment with which his force fought a major battle. (IWM)

HOW THE FORCES COMPARED

Royal Air Force, 1 July 1940
Aircraft in Fighter Command Squadrons
Single-engined fighters:

Spitfires	286
Hurricanes	463
Defiants	37
Twin-engined fighters (Blenheims)	114
TOTAL	**900**

Luftwaffe, 20 July 1940
Aircraft in Air Fleets 2, 3 and 5
Fighters:

Single-engined (Me 109s)	844
Twin-engined (Me 110s)	250
Bombers:	
Single-engined (Ju 87s)	280
Twin-engined (Do 17s, Ju 88s, He 111s)	1,330
Long-Range Reconnaissance:	80
TOTAL	**2,784**

The preparations for such a 'landing operation' were to be completed early in August and the role for the Luftwaffe was simply stated:

'The English Air Force must be so reduced, morally and physically, that it is unable to deliver any significant attack against an invasion across the Channel.'

Yet even now the German leader did not think an invasion would be necessary. If his air force could deliver a series of sufficiently powerful blows on the enemy homeland he expected the British, like his previous enemies, to prostrate themselves at his feet.

In July the Luftwaffe began a series of small-scale actions over the English Channel, aimed at disrupting British shipping passing through the waterway and forcing the Royal Air Force into battle to defend them. Steadily the air fighting over the Channel became more ferocious, and the Germans began sending free hunting patrols to engage RAF fighters over southern England.

Typical of the scrappy actions of the period was that on the afternoon of 13 July, when a convoy of freighters passed through the Strait of Dover. Half-a-dozen Junkers 87s from Dive-Bomber Geschwader 1 dived to bomb the ships, and came under attack from eleven Hurricanes of No 56 Squadron. Major Josef Foezoe, leading a Staffel of Me 109s, described what happened next:

'Unfortunately for them [the Hurricanes], they slid into position directly between the Stukas and our close-escort Messerschmitts. We opened fire, and at once three Hurricanes separated from the formation, two dropping and one gliding down to the water smoking heavily. At that instant I saw a Stuka diving in an attempt to reach the French coast. It was chased by a single Hurricane. Behind the Hurricane was a 109, and behind that, a second Hurricane, all of the fighters firing at the aircraft in front. I saw the deadly dangerous situation and rushed down. There were five aircraft diving in a line towards the water. The Stuka was badly hit and both crewmen wounded; it crashed on the beach near Wissant. The leading Messerschmitt, flown by Feldwebel John, shot down the first Hurricane into the water, its right wing appeared above the waves like the dorsal fin of a shark before it sank. My Hurricane dropped like a stone close to the one that John had shot down.'

Air Vice-Marshal Keith Park, commander of No 11 Group that bore the brunt of the fighting over southern England. A 48-year-old New Zealander who had flown fighters over France during the First World War, he was a devout Christian who drew great strength from his religion. His air defence fiefdom comprised the whole of south-eastern England, to a line running approximately from Southampton, via Aylesbury, to Lowestoft. Flying his personal Hurricane, Park frequently visited his squadrons to gain a first-hand impression of the progress of the Battle. An energetic and popular leader, Park had the rare gift of being able to make those around him feel that their views mattered. (IWM)

Reichsmarschall Hermann Goering, 47, (centre) had been Commander-in-Chief of the Luftwaffe since it began its expansion in 1933. He was a successful fighter pilot during the First World War, and at the end of the conflict he commanded the famous Richthofen Geschwader. After the war he played a leading part in the formation of the Nazi party. By 1940 he was at the height of his political power and had been designated by Hitler as his successor. Though he is often characterized as a rotund buffoon with a vanity for dressing up, Goering could be astute and ruthless when the occasion demanded. He is seen here with staff officers during a visit of inspection to the Channel Coast in September 1940.

Generalfeldmarschall Albert Kesselring, 45, (second from left) was commander of Air Fleet 2 during the Battle. During the First World War he served in the Army and rose to become adjutant of a brigade. An extremely capable administrator, he transferred to the new Luftwaffe when it formed in 1933 and became head of that service's Administrative Office. In the years that followed he held a succession of progressively more important posts and in the summer of 1940 commanded Air Fleet 2, the largest Air Fleet. From his headquarters in Brussels he directed Luftwaffe units based in Holland, Belgium and in France as far west as the Seine. A German officer of the old school, Kesselring had a ready smile, was firm but always courteous to subordinates and was greatly respected by them. To the left of Kesselring is

General Jeschonnek, Chief of Staff of the Luftwaffe. On his right are General Speidel, Chief of Staff of Air fleet 2, and General Loerzer who commanded the IInd Air Corps.

Right: Generalfeldmarschall Hugo Sperrle, 55, commander of Luftflotte 3. During the Battle his headquarters were in Paris from which he commanded Luftwaffe units based west of the Seine. During the

First World War he had served in the Imperial Flying Service, and transferred to the Army after the conflict. In 1935 he moved to the new Luftwaffe and the following year was appointed to command the Condor Legion, the Luft-

waffe contingent sent to fight in the Spanish Civil War. In contrast to Kesselring, Sperrle was an aloof figure and a stickler for protocol. Hitler referred to him as one of his 'most brutal-looking generals'. (Bundesarchiv)

No 56 Squadron lost two Hurricanes destroyed and two damaged. Two Ju 87s were seriously damaged; Geschwader 51 had no losses.

Six days later, on 19 July, nine Defiants of No 141 Squadron were scrambled from Hawkinge to intercept an enemy force approaching one of the convoys. The Defiant, a two-seater with its armament of four machine-guns mounted in a turret, was designed to engage unescorted bomber formations; it had not been designed to dogfight with enemy single-seaters. Soon after they left the coast near Folkestone the Defiants were 'bounced' by Messerschmitt 109s of Fighter Geschwader 51. Two of the British fighters were immediately shot down and during the subsequent dogfight the inferiority of the turret fighter for this sort of action was clearly demonstrated. By attacking from behind and below, the Messerschmitts kept outside the Defiant's return fire, and the two-seaters lacked the speed or manoeuvrability to avoid these tactics.

Twelve Hurricanes from No 111 Squadron were sent to assist the Defiants, but arrived only in time to save the two-seaters from

complete annihilation. Of the nine Defiants only three survived, and one of those was damaged. Of the eighteen men in the Defiants, ten were killed and two wounded. Only one Messerschmitt was shot down. For Air Chief Marshal Dowding the lessons of the 19 July action were clear enough, and within two days both his Defiant squadrons were on their way to quiet areas in the north where they would be safe from enemy single-seaters.

A further lesson during the early engagements was that the German fighter sweeps were inflicting unacceptably severe losses on British fighter units. RAF Sector controllers received orders to vector fighters only against those enemy formations thought to contain bombers; whenever possible the enemy fighter sweeps were to be left alone. For the Luftwaffe the early actions brought the clear lesson that unescorted bombers operating by day over southern England could expect short shrift if they were caught by British fighters.

Inexorably the pace of fighting continued to accelerate. On 8 August there was a fierce air battle around convoy 'Peewit' in the Channel and out of twenty ships, four were sunk and six

Hans-Jurgen Stumpff, commander of Air Fleet 5 based in Norway and Denmark. Following its disastrous intervention on 15 August, Luftflotte 5 played little further part in the Battle.

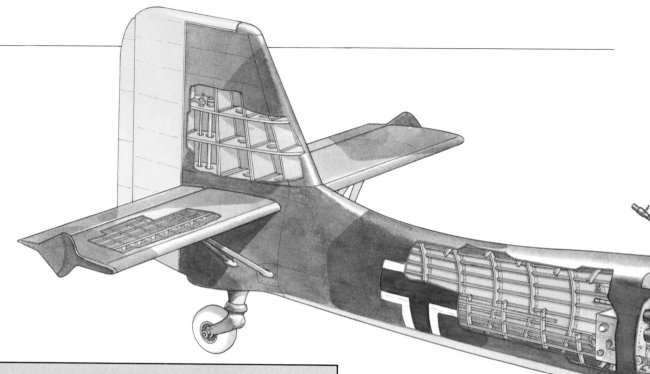

damaged. In actions around the convoy the Luftwaffe lost 28 aircraft and Fighter Command lost 19. On 11 August the Luftwaffe launched its first large-scale attack on a target in Britain. Following feints by fighters in the Dover area, a force of about 70 Heinkel 111s and Junkers 88s, escorted by nearly 100 Messerschmitt 109s and 110s, made for the naval base at Portland. Eight squadrons of Spitfires and Hurricanes were scrambled to intercept and in the ensuing action the Luftwaffe lost 40 aircraft; the RAF lost 26 fighters.

On 12 August there was a similar heavy attack, this time against Portsmouth, as well as subsidiary attacks by dive-bombers against several targets including the Chain Home radar stations at Pevensey, Rye, Dover, Dunkirk (in Kent) and Ventnor. These radar stations were small pinpoint targets, however, and proved difficult to hit and even more

difficult to put out of action for any length of time. Following hasty repairs, all the radar stations except that at Ventnor were operating the following day.

During the 34-day period of skirmishes between 10 July and 12 August, the Luftwaffe lost 261 aircraft and Fighter Command 127. This gave a loss ratio of just over 2:1 in favour of the Royal Air Force, but this had been during a period of small-scale actions as the two sides felt out each other's strengths and weaknesses. The average total daily loss for both sides had been eleven aircraft, and the scale of the actions put neither air force to any real test. On 2 August orders were issued to the Luftwaffe's Air Fleets 2, 3 and 5 to begin a series of all-out attacks aimed at destroying RAF Fighter Command as an effective fighting force. The new phase of the German attack was to begin on 13 August.

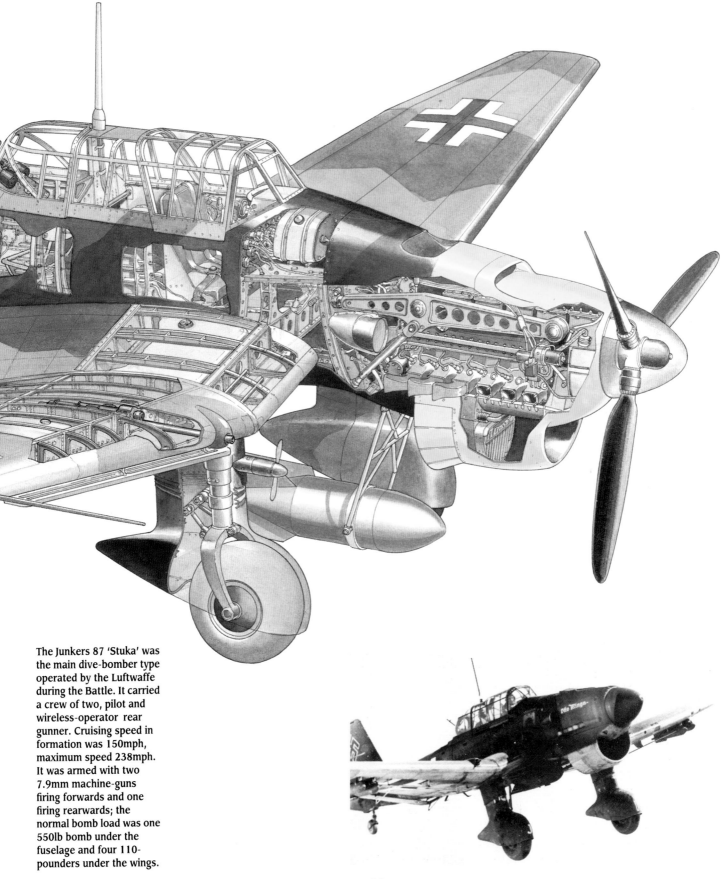

The Junkers 87 'Stuka' was the main dive-bomber type operated by the Luftwaffe during the Battle. It carried a crew of two, pilot and wireless-operator rear gunner. Cruising speed in formation was 150mph, maximum speed 238mph. It was armed with two 7.9mm machine-guns firing forwards and one firing rearwards; the normal bomb load was one 550lb bomb under the fuselage and four 110-pounders under the wings.

The Luftwaffe's New Opponent

Oberleutnant Julius Neumann, Me 109 pilot, Fighter Geschwader 27

'During the campaign in France it was difficult to compare our Me 109 with the French Morane or Curtiss fighters, because I never had a dogfight with either of them. I saw only one Morane during the entire campaign and it was disappearing in the distance. Our Geschwader had very little dogfighting experience until the Dunkirk action, where we met the Royal Air Force for the first time in numbers. Our pilots came back with the highest respect for the enemy. I personally did not experience dogfighting until early in August, when I became embroiled with British fighters over the Isle of Wight. And we felt we were dealing with a pilot-plane combination as good as our own. The longer-serving RAF pilots had considerable flying experience, they were well trained and they knew what they were fighting for. Of course there were young and inexperienced pilots too, but we had the feeling that there was a backbone of very well-trained and experienced pilots.'

Oberleutnant Julius Neumann of Fighter Geschwader 27.

◄
The Heinkel 59 floatplane, an obsolete torpedo bomber, served in the air-sea rescue role during the Battle. (via Schliephake)

Focke-Wulf 200 Condor of Bomber Geschwader 40. This unit flew long-range anti-shipping missions into the Atlantic round the west of the British Isles, flying between bases at Bordeaux in France and Trondheim in Norway. (Kowalewski)

Scenes at the fighter airfield at Caffiers near Calais, home of the IIIrd Gruppe of Fighter Geschwader 26 during the Battle of Britain, showing the unit's Me 109s in their sandbagged and camouflaged revetments. (Schoepfel)

Aircrew of Bomber Geschwader 76 trying out one of the rubber dinghies issued to the unit, as part of the preparation for over-water missions against Britain. (Rehm)

The Messerschmitt 109E was the sole single-engined fighter type operated by the Luftwaffe during the Battle of Britain. It had a maximum speed of 354mph. The usual armament was two 20mm cannon and two 7.9mm machine-guns. The type also served in the fighter-bomber role, carrying up to 550lb of bombs. ▼

The Bristol Blenheim was the main long-range and night fighter type in Fighter Command throughout the Battle. The version depicted, the Mark IV, had a maximum speed of 266mph – too slow to catch up with enemy bombers if the element of surprise had been lost and they began evasive manoeuvres. The Blenheim carried five 0.303in machine-guns firing forwards and one more in the fuselage turret. The example depicted carries airborne interception (AI) rader, with aerials protruding from the extreme nose and the leading edge of the starboard wing, and above and below the port wing. ▶

The Dornier 17 remained in large-scale service in the Luftwaffe throughout the Battle, although production had ceased and it was being replaced by the Ju 88. Normal crew of four was: pilot, navigator/bomb-aimer/front gunner, wireless-operator/rear gunner and flight engineer/ventral gunner; sometimes a fifth man was carried to operate the guns firing from each side of the cabin. Cruising speed, in formation was 190mph, maximum speed 265mph. Armed with up to five 7.9mm machine-guns, the Do 17 had a bomb load of up to 2,200lb. These machines belonged to Bomber Geschwader 76. (Rehm) ▼

► Adolf Hitler discussing the air fighting with Major Werner Moelders, the commander of Fighter Geschwader 51. Having emerged from the Spanish Civil War as the top-scoring German fighter pilot, Moelders retained this distinction throughout the Battle of Britain and achieved his fortieth victory on 29 September.

Silent sentinels. The Chain Home radar station at Swingate near Dover, showing the 350ft-high towers carrying the receiver aerials. Although the towers appeared fragile, the openwork structures presented a small area to blast or fragmentation effects and were difficult to knock down.

Observer Corps Post. Manned by civilian volunteers, a web of these posts tracked enemy formations once they had crossed the coast and were heading inland. (IWM)

The King inspecting WAAFs at Kenley. WAAFs played a vitally important part in the fighter control organization during the Battle.

Heinkel 115 floatplane of Coastal Patrol Gruppe 506. During the Battle this unit was based in Norway and northern Germany, conducting night minelaying operations off ports. (via Schliephake)

The New Pilot

Sergeant Harry Newton, Hurricane pilot, No 111 Squadron

'When I arrived from Croydon after training the CO asked me how many hours I had on the Hurricane. I said I had fifteen. He said "That's no good to me. You will fly three hours each morning and two each afternoon until you have 45 hours on type."

'When I had the 45 hours on the Hurricane I was called in front of the CO for a ten-minute lecture on how to fight the Hun. It was all high falutin' stuff, delivered while I stood in front of him to attention with my hat on. He said things like "The Hun is a very tricky chap, Newton. You've got to be very wary." The only thing I got out of the interview was that when I was flying alone and the enemy was around, I was not to fly straight for more than two seconds. At the end of the chat the CO said, "You've done 45 hours' flying on the Hurricane, as from tomorrow you will be Blue 3."

'Gradually I gained experience in formation flying, operational scrambles, etc. My biggest worry was falling away from the fight and being called a coward.'

Smoke rising over Dover harbour, from a fire started during the dive-bomber attack on the port on the morning of 29 July.

Hawker Hurricane of No 56 Squadron. The most numerous fighter type in the Royal Air Force during the Battle, the Hurricane equipped thirty-six squadrons. Carrying the armour and equipment fitted at that time, its maximum speed was 328mph. Standard armament was eight 0.303in machine-guns. (Pathé)

The Spitfire – a German Assessment

Oberleutnant Hans Schmoller-Haldy, Me 109 pilot, Fighter Geschwader 54

'I was able to fly a captured Spitfire at Jever. My first impression was that it had a beautiful engine. It purred. The engine of the Messerschmitt 109 was very loud. Also the Spitfire was easier to fly, and to land, than the Me 109. The 109 was unforgiving of any inattention. I felt familiar with the Spitfire from the very start. That was my first and lasting impression. But with my experience with the 109, I personally would not have traded it for a Spitfire. I had the impression, though I did not fly the Spitfire long enough to prove it, that the 109 was the faster, especially in the dive. Also, I think the pilot's view was better from the 109. In the Spitfire one flew further back, a bit more over the wing.

'For fighter-versus-fighter combat, I thought the Spitfire was better armed than the Me 109. The cannon fitted to the 109 were not much use against enemy fighters, and the machine-guns on top of the engine often suffered stoppages. The cannon were good if they scored a hit, but their rate of fire was very low. The cannon had greater range than the machine-guns. But we were always told that in a dogfight one could not hope to hit anything at ranges greater than 50 metres, it was necessary to close in to short range.'

The Supermarine Spitfire, the highest-performance fighter type in the Royal Air Force, equipped nineteen squadrons during the Battle. Carrying the equipment and armour standard on aircraft in the summer of 1940, the Mark I had a maximum speed of 345mph. The Mark II, which entered service that September, had a more powerful engine and a maximum speed of 354mph. Standard arma- ment was eight 0.303in machine-guns, but a few Spitfires took part in the Battle modified to carry two 20mm cannon.

THE INITIAL SKIRMISHES – AIRCRAFT LOSSES

This section lists the aircraft lost or damaged beyond repair in combat missions during each 24-hour period. In the case of the Luftwaffe, losses of all types of aircraft engaged in operations against Britain are listed. In the case of the RAF the list gives fighters lost in the air or on the ground.

	Luftwaffe	RAF	Action
10 July	12	3	Heavy attack on shipping
11 July	16	6	Heavy attacks on ports and shipping
12 July	8	3	Attacks on ports and shipping
13 July	6	2	Attacks on shipping
14 July	3	1	Attack on shipping
15 July	3	1	Attack on shipping
16 July	3	0	Bad weather restricted flying
17 July	2	1	Poor weather, attack on shipping
18 July	4	5	Attacks on ports and shipping
19 July	5	10	Attack on Dover
20 July	10	8	Attacks on shipping
21 July	8	2	Attacks on shipping
22 July	1	1	Attacks on ports and shipping
23 July	2	0	Attacks on shipping and other targets
24 July	10	3	Attacks on shipping
25 July	13	6	Heavy attacks on shipping
26 July	3	1	Poor weather, little activity
27 July	4	2	Attacks on shipping
28 July	10	2	Attacks on ports and shipping
29 July	12	5	Attacks on shipping
30 July	6	0	Attacks on shipping
31 July	3	3	Attacks on shipping
1 August	7	3	Attacks on shipping
2 August	4	0	Attacks on shipping
3 August	4	0	Attacks on shipping
4 August	0	0	Little activity
5 August	3	1	Attacks on shipping
6 August	0	0	Little activity
7 August	1	0	Attacks on shipping
8 August	28	19	Large-scale attacks on convoy
9 August	4	0	Little activity
10 August	0	0	Little activity
11 August	40	26	Heavy attacks on shipping and Portland
12 August	26	13	Attacks on shipping and radar stations
TOTALS	**261**	**127**	

Messerschmitt 109 pilots of III FG 26. From left to right: Leutnant Luedewig, Leutnant Heinz Ebeling, Oberleutnant Gerhard Schoepfel, Oberleutnant Josef Haiboeck and Leutnant Hans Nauman. (Schoepfel)

Far left: Hauptmann Karl Ebbinghausen, commander of the IInd Gruppe of FG 26, in his Messerschmitt 109. Ebbinghausen was killed in action on 16 August.

◄ Leutnant Rudolf Ahrens, a Heinkel 111 pilot of BG 1, was shot down and captured on 18 August. (Ahrens)

Far left: Major Helmut Bode, Junkers 87 pilot and commander of IIIrd Gruppe Dive Bomber Geschwader 77. (Bode)

◄ Pilots of the 3rd Staffel, Erprobungsgruppe 210, pictured shortly before the opening of the Battle of Britain. This unit operated in the fighter-bomber role and suffered heavy losses. (Hintze)

Squadron Leader Douglas Bader, the famous pilot who had had both legs amputated following a flying accident before the war, commanded No 242 Squadron and led the Duxford 'Big Wing' during the Battle. (IWM)

▶
Pilot Officer 'Dutch' Hugo, a South African, served with No 615 Squadron.

Far right:
Squadron Leader Robert Stanford-Tuck, CO of No 257 Squadron. (IWM)

▶
Lieutenant A. 'The Admiral' Blake was one of several Fleet Air Arm pilots transferred to Fighter Command from the Admiralty in July 1940. He flew with No 19 Squadron, and was killed in action on 29 October.

Far right:
Flying Officer 'Uncle Sam' Leckrone, an American volunteer, fought during the Battle with Nos 616 and 19 Squadrons. Later he became a founder member of No 71, the first U.S. 'Eagle' Squadron. (IWM)

Flight Sergeant Phil Tew, No 54 Squadron. (Tew)

Flying Officer John Hardacre of No 504 Squadron, killed in action on 30 September. (No 504 Sqn Association)

Sergeant Herbert Hallowes, No 43 Squadron (Hallowes).

Flying Officer Stefan Witorzenc, a Pole, flew with No 501 Squadron.

Boulton Paul Defiants of No 264 Squadron, the first unit to receive this type. The Defiant carried its armament of four 0.303in machine-guns in the turret amidships, and the fighter was designed to engage unescorted enemy bomber formations. Its maximum speed was 304mph. During the Battle the Defiant units suffered heavy losses whenever they encountered Messerschmitt 109s, and at the end of August the type was relegated to night operations. (IWM)

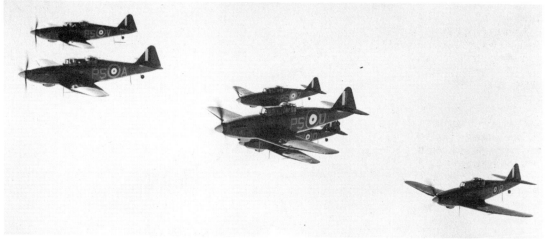

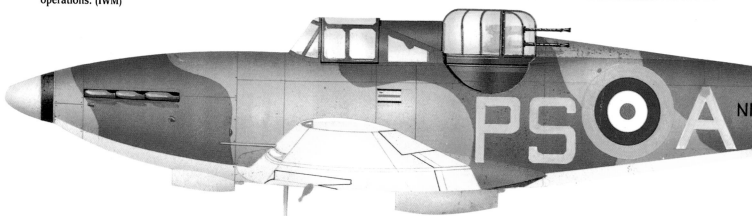

These ungainly hydrogen-filled gasbags were 62ft long and 25ft in diameter, and had a maximum effective altitude of about 5,000ft. They were dotted randomly over the target to be defended and were intended as a deterrent against low-flying aircraft and to prevent dive-bombers pressing their attacks to low altitude. If an aircraft struck the cable, explosive cutters severed the wire at the top and the bottom, allowing the bomber to carry the cable away. Attached to either end of the cable was an 8ft-diameter canvas drogue; when fully open, the drogues exerted a combined drag of 7 tons at 200mph – sufficient to stop an aircraft in its tracks and send it spinning out of control. The main balloon-defended areas in south-east England were at London, Chatham and Dover, Harwich, Portsmouth, Gosport and Southampton.

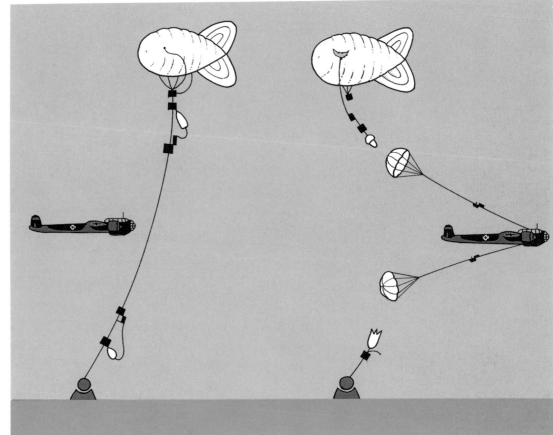

▶
A barrage balloon flying from the grassed area immediately to the south of the Houses of Parliament. (IWM)

▶
Shooting down barrage balloons became a popular pastime for Messerschmitt pilots with time on their hands. Here balloons are seen going down on fire at Gosport. (McKee)

The Ground Crews

Squadron Leader Michael Crossley, Commander of No 32 Squadron

'The ground crews were past all praise. If we had long hours, they had longer ones by far. They were always laughing and ragging round the place and betting cigarettes or drinks as to whether "A" Flight would do better than "B" Flight or whether such and such a pilot would get one or two today.

'How Tubby, the Squadron Engineer Officer, continued to render at least fifteen out of about twenty Hurricanes serviceable at every readiness period is a secret that will die with him. A lot of publicity and glamour comes the way of the fighter pilot but not all the praise in the world would do justice to these "back-room boys".'

Feldwebel Horst Schultz, Dornier Do 17 pilot, Bomber Geschwader 3

'Each Staffel had its own dispersal area around the perimeter of the airfield at Antwerp. When we arrived the Dornier's engines had been warmed up and my mechanic, Gefreiter Erich Treder, said "Machine Cleared!" I did not do a walk-round check of the aircraft. If Treder said an aircraft was cleared for flight that was as good as a gold-stamped guarantee.'

In many cases German units operated from hastily prepared airfields and most servicing work, including engine changes, had to be done in the open.

▲
Work on a Messerschmitt 109 at Caffiers. (Schoepfel)

▶
Work on a Messerschmitt 110 at Laval.

During the Battle both sides depended on the ability of their ground crews to carry out rapid turn-arounds, refuel, rearm and rectify faults on the fighters quickly, so that they were ready to go into action again.

◄ Far left:
Spitfire of No 92 Squadron being refuelled from a Crossley tanker, probably at Biggin Hill. (IWM)

◄
Spitfire of No 66 Squadron being rearmed at Gravesend. Each box was pre-loaded with 300 rounds of 0.303in ammunition. (Times Newspapers)

▲
A four-gun battery of the 52nd Heavy Anti-Aircraft Regiment, in position near Barking. The 4.5in gun was the latest and heaviest anti-aircraft weapon used by the Royal Artillery during the Battle, and fired 55lb shells at a rate of eight per minute.

Bofors 40mm light anti-aircraft gun. This weapon fired 2lb shells at a rate of 120 per minute, and could be lethally effective against low-flying aircraft. Far too few Bofors guns were available to defend airfields and other vital points during the summer of 1940, however. (IWM)
▶

BATTLE OF BRITAIN FIGHTER TACTICS

At the beginning of the Second World War few air forces had a clear idea of how, or even if, their fighters would engage those of the enemy. In each case the fighters had been designed primarily to engage enemy bombers, and many experts believed that the increases in performance since the First World War had made dogfighting a thing of the past. The Royal Air Force Manual of Air Tactics, 1938 edition, solemnly stated:

'Manoeuvre at high speeds in air fighting is not now practicable, because the effect of gravity on the human body during rapid changes of direction at high speed causes a temporary loss of consciousness, deflection shooting becomes difficult and accuracy is hard to obtain.'

As a result RAF fighter tactics were designed to defeat formations of bombers, and the possibility of fighter-versus-fighter combat was almost ignored.

To engage a formation of bombers effectively it was necessary to employ the concentrated fire power of a large number of fighters. Thus the RAF planned to use a squadron formation of twelve aircraft, divided into four sections each of three aircraft. During cruising flight the sections flew in V formation, the commander flew in the middle of the leading V and the other three Vs flew behind in close line astern.

The fighters flew close together with about one wing span, 12 yards, between them. As well as giving concentrated fire power, this type of formation was best for the penetration of cloud – an important factor to be considered in air operations over northern Europe.

The squadron commander was to lead his formation to a position on the flank of the enemy bomber formation. Once there he ordered his sections into echelon, and took his own section in to attack. Each fighter pilot was to move into a firing position behind an enemy bomber where (again in the words of the 1938 RAF Manual of Air Tactics):

' . . . he stays until either he has exhausted his ammunition, the target aircraft has been shot down, or he himself has been shot down or his engine put out of action.'

The other sections were to queue up behind the leader's, and attack in turn after the section in front had broken away. This tactical formation and type of attack was not the only one in use in the RAF, but it was representative of the rigid tactical thinking in this air force and many others before the war.

In 1939 the only evidence available to most air forces on the nature of modern air warfare was what could be gleaned from reports on the Spanish Civil War. Studying

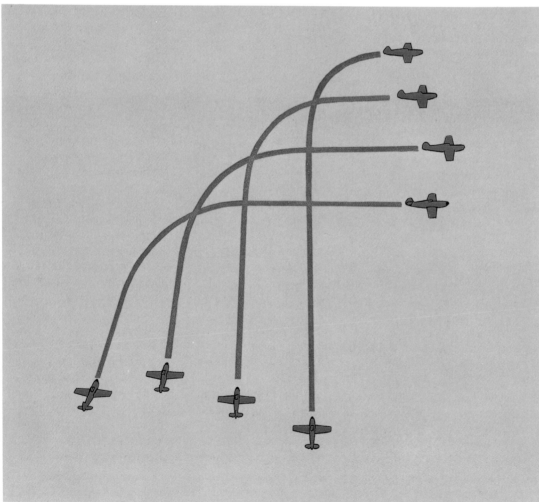

Above: The Sandwich Manoeuvre. By means of a simple turn, an attacking aircraft would be sandwiched between its intended victim and the aircraft next to it in formation.

▶
A Spitfire squadron flying in close Vics of threes, the standard formation used by the RAF up to the middle of 1940. (RAF Museum)

Left: The Cross-over Turn, which enabled each aircraft to hold position in the formation during a tight turn maintaining high speed.

▶
Messerschmitt 109s of Fighter Geschwader 27, flying in the open *Schwarm* formation. (Neumann)

BATTLE OF BRITAIN FIGHTER TACTICS

such reports was like perusing the Bible: no matter what one was trying to prove, one was almost certain to find evidence to support it. The conflict in Spain had shown that the bombers almost always got through to their targets, and if conditions were favourable they could cause severe damage. There had been a great deal of scrappy fighter-versus-fighter combat, but most of it was inconclusive and little of it was between fighters of modern design.

Only in Germany were the lessons of the Spanish Civil War put to good use. The Luftwaffe emerged from the conflict with no doubt that air combat between modern fighters, although difficult, was likely to occur in any future war. Over Spain the German pilots had experimented there with a novel set of tactics for fighters based on the *Rotte,* or widely spaced pair of aircraft. During cruising flight the two aircraft flew about 200 yards apart, almost in line abreast with the leader slightly ahead; each pilot concentrated his search inwards to cover his partner's blind area behind and below. During combat against enemy fighters the wing-man kept watch for enemy aircraft attacking from behind, allowing the leader to concentrate on the enemy planes he was going after.

Two *Rotten* made up a *Schwarm* of four aircraft, with the leading *Rotte* to one side and slightly ahead of the other, and the aircraft were stepped down into the sun. With its component aircraft spaced about 200 yards apart, the *Schwarm* formation was approximately 600 yards wide, making it almost impossible for the aircraft to hold position during a tight turn at high speed. The answer was the 'cross-over' turn: each aircraft turned as tightly as it could, and swapped sides in the formation.

In determining the effectiveness of a combat formation for fighters, three factors need to be considered: first, the ability of the formation to manoeuvre while maintaining cohesion; secondly, the ability of the pilots to cover each others' blind areas and thus prevent a surprise attack on any of the aircraft; and, thirdly, the ability of each aircraft in the formation to receive rapid support from the others if it came under attack. On each of these three criteria, the German tactical formations were greatly superior to the tight formation used by the RAF. Using the 'cross-over' turn, the *Schwarm* could turn as tightly as individual aircraft were able; in the tight formations used by the RAF, the rate of turn was limited by the need to fly round the aircraft on the inside of the 'V'. In cruising flight, every pilot in a *Schwarm* searched for the enemy, and each man was positioned to see into his comrades' blind areas. In the tight formations used by the RAF, only the leader searched for the enemy while the other pilots concentrated on holding formation. Thus there was poor coverage of the all-important sector behind and below the formation. If an aircraft in a *Rotte* or a *Schwarm* was attacked from behind, a simple turn would result in the attacker being 'sand-wiched'; if the rear section of a tight formation came under attack, the action was usually over before others in the formation could come to its aid.

Over France and during the early part of the Battle of Britain, the RAF's fighters were tactically outclassed by their German counterparts. The middle of a battle is no place for a radical change in tactics, and the RAF had to make the best use it could of the tactics in which its pilots had been trained. The V formation was widened out to allow pilots to spend more time searching for the enemy rather than holding an exact distance from their neighbours; and one section, led by an experienced pilot, flew a weaving course about 1,000 feet above the main formation, keeping watch for the enemy to prevent surprise attack. These two steps greatly improved the search and mutual support capabilities of the fighter formation, although they did little to improve its ability to turn tightly without losing cohesion.

It remained to be seen whether these changes would allow RAF fighters to engage those of the Luftwaffe on equal terms.

2. ASSAULT ON THE AIRFIELDS
13 August to 6 September

'Their force is wonderful, great and strong, yet we pluck their feathers by little and little.'
Sir William Howard, 'Of the Spanish Armada'

THE ACTIONS IN JULY and the early part of August were only a prelude to the main thrust by the Luftwaffe, and it was on 13 August that the battle, in German eyes, really began. On that day the Luftwaffe launched a total of 1,485 sorties against Britain, hitting the naval base at Portland and the port of Southampton as well as the airfields at Detling and Eastchurch. During the day's battles the Luftwaffe lost 39 aircraft and the RAF lost 14.

On the next day, the 14th, the Luftwaffe mounted attacks on several airfields, though with rather less aircraft. On the 15th the Luftwaffe returned in force, with large-scale attacks on several airfields and radar stations. From its bases in Norway and Denmark, Air Fleet 5 sent Heinkel 111s and Junkers 88s escorted by Me 110s to attack targets in northern England, hoping to catch Fighter Command off balance. In this the raiders failed utterly – the attacking forces were all intercepted and suffered heavy losses as a result. In the course of the various actions that day the Luftwaffe lost 79 aircraft while the RAF lost 34. Thereafter Air Fleet 5 played little further part in the battle and many of its units were transferred to Air Fleet 2 and 3 based in France, Holland and Belgium.

Thus began the series of large-scale hard-fought actions that was to continue with few breaks over the next six weeks. Each of the actions contained features unique to itself and it would be misleading to describe any of them as typical. Nevertheless the series of engagements fought on Sunday, 18 August fit well into the broad pattern of those of the initial phase of the battle, and will serve to illustrate the variety in the methods of attack employed by the German bomber force as well as the defensive tactics used by Fighter Command. We shall, therefore, examine that day's events in detail.

In the No 11 Group Plotting Room at Uxbridge

Aircraftwoman Vera Saies, plotter, Uxbridge

'The whole thing could be best described as "organized chaos." When things got going plots from the filter room were coming through at about five per minute on each track. The room pictured the scene of battle with raids on the table, and the squadron boards showing the information given by our controller whose voice boomed out continually. Girls would be calling for new counters to update their blocks, runners would be dashing to get them from the table beside the plotting map. If one asked for one thing and one's neighbour asked for something else, it was a matter of who shouted loudest! It was all so unlike the quiet, relaxed atmosphere often depicted in films. Looking down on us from behind the soundproof glass were the duty fighter controller and his assistants. They seemed so calm, so removed from the hubbub below; if things there had been as chaotic as they were with us, I don't think we could have won the battle.'

For 18 August, the Luftwaffe had planned an ambitious programme of attacks aimed at the four most important British fighter airfields in south-eastern England: Biggin Hill, Kenley, Hornchurch and North Weald. These airfields were further inland than any previously attacked on a large scale. In addition, a large force of Stukas (Ju 87s) was to attack airfields and a radar station in the Portsmouth area. Thus the stage was set for the action that would see the destruction of more aircraft than in any other day during the Battle of Britain – 'The Hardest Day.'

It was a beautiful summer's day, with blue skies and just a few puffs of cloud. The morning began quietly enough, with single German reconnaissance aircraft making fleet-ing high-altitude incursions over southern England to take photographs and report on the weather. From time to time British fighters were scrambled to intercept these intruders, but the latter proved difficult targets and only one was shot down.

The first large-scale attack opened shortly after noon, when the radar stations in south-eastern England began reporting concentra-tions of enemy aircraft assembling over the

Pas de Calais area. In the vanguard of the raiding force were 39 Dornier 17s and Junkers 88s of Bomber Geschwader 76 flying at 12,000 feet and bound for Kenley airfield. Also, as yet unseen on the British radar, were nine more Dorniers of the 9th Staffel of BG 76 flying just above the waves; these aircraft were to deliver a surprise attack on Kenley from low altitude. About 15 miles behind the leading high-altitude raiding force came a second large force comprising 60 Heinkel 111s of Bomber Geschwader 1, making for Biggin Hill airfield. Escorting the high-flying bombers were more than 150 Messerschmitt 109 and Me 110 fighters.

From their underground operations room at Uxbridge, the controllers of No 11 Group, Fighter Command, disposed their squadrons to contest the enemy incursion. One squadron with twelve Hurricanes, No 501, was already airborne moving from one base to another; it received orders to climb into position to meet the enemy. Within minutes eight further squadrons had been scrambled and were moving into blocking positions ahead of the raiders.

By 1 pm the fighters assigned to intercept the raiders were all airborne and clawing for altitude as they moved into position. Five squadrons with 53 Spitfires and Hurricanes were moving to patrol the line Canterbury – Margate to block any possible attack aimed at the port installations along the Thames Estuary or the fighter airfields to the north of it. As they did so four more squadrons, with 50 Spitfires and Hurricanes, were spiralling up into position to cover their bases at Kenley and Biggin Hill.

The first clash took place over Canterbury and the defenders got the worst of it. Ober-leutnant Gerhard Schoepfel was leading a formation of Messerschmitt 109s of Fighter Geschwader 26 on a free hunting patrol when he came upon the Hurricanes of No 501 Squadron in the climb. Ordering the others to remain at altitude and give him cover should he need it, Schoepfel went down to engage the enemy alone. Unseen, he sneaked in behind the Hurricanes and shot down four in rapid succession before his own fighter was struck by debris from the last of his victims and he was forced to break off the action. Schoepfel

◄
The author standing outside the entrance to No 11 Group's underground operations room at Uxbridge.

Inside the operations room at Uxbridge.
◄
The controllers' gallery seen from the floor of the room.
►
The situation map as seen from the controllers' gallery.

◄ The King awarding the DSO and the DFC to Squadron Leader Joseph Kayll, commander of No 615 Squadron based at Kenley.

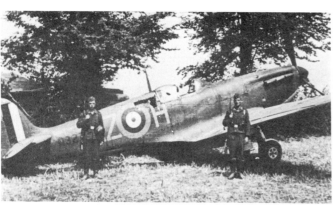

▲ Spitfire of No 234 Squadron guarded by German troops after it was forced down near Cherbourg on 15 August. The pilot was taken prisoner.

◄ Junkers 88 taking off for an attack. The aircraft carries a 1,100lb bomb on the starboard external rack, and a 550-pounder on the port rack.

The Heinkel 111 was the main twin-engined bomber type used by the Luftwaffe during the Battle. Normally it carried a crew of four: pilot, navigator/bomb-aimer/front gunner, radio-operator rear gunner and flight engineer/ventral gunner. Sometimes a fifth man was carried to operate the guns firing from each side of the fuselage. Cruising speed in forma-tion was 190mph, maxi-mum speed 258mph. It carried an armament of up to six 7.9mm machine-guns in separate mountings, and a bomb load of up to 3,300lb.

had carried through a brilliant engagement, and one that illustrated that, although the RAF had improved its tactics, they still had shortcomings.

By luck rather than design, both formations of high-altitude bombers passed just out of sight of the main British fighter concentration in the Canterbury – Margate area. The bomber crews saw nothing of the defending fighters until they reached Sevenoaks, when they ran into four squadrons positioned to defend Biggin Hill and Kenley. Then the action began in earnest.

The commander of No 32 Squadron, Squadron Leader Mike Crossley, sighted the incoming enemy formation several miles away, and positioned his Hurricanes for a head-on attack. Raimund Schultz, a war correspondent in one of the Dorniers, afterwards wrote of the subsequent attack: 'Here comes the first fighter, from the left and ahead. Very suddenly he is before our eyes, like a wasp, dashing through our formation. I see the reddish tracer rounds flying back and forth. Everything happens very quickly.'

In one of the Hurricanes, Pilot Officer Alan Eckford loosed off a short burst at one of the Dorniers, then had to push hard on his stick to avoid colliding with it. Once past his victim he looked back and saw the bomber pull up in a drunken half roll, then spin away to earth. Lying on his stomach on the floor of the Dornier and manning the rearwards-firing machine-gun, Oberfeldwebel Wilhelm Lautersack had heard a crash as Eckford's rounds rammed into the bomber. Then the aircraft began to spin and he was pinned to the floor by the vicious G forces. Lautersack glanced forwards, to see his pilot slumped lifeless against his harness. With a strength born of fear the German crewman inched his way to the escape hatch in the floor of the cabin, pulled the lever to release it, and tumbled out. After a long delay he pulled his ripcord and was relieved when the canopy opened with a loud 'thwack.'

Meanwhile Donald MacDonell at the head of No 64 Squadron was leading his Spitfires down from above to engage the German formation. 'I gave a quick call "Freema Squadron, Bandits below! Tally Ho!" Then down we went in a wide spiral, keeping a wary eye open for the

▶ Bomb damage at Manston, the only Fighter Command airfield to be put out of action for any length of time during the Battle. The wrecked aircraft was a Magister trainer.

◀ A Gruppe of Dornier 17s flying in typical attack formation. (Schoepfel) ▼

◀ Hurricane seen breaking away, after attacking a Junkers 88.

◀ Taken on the afternoon of 16 August from a Dornier 17 of BG 76, this photo shows ten Hurricanes climbing into position before delivering their attack. Almost certainly the fighters belonged to No 111 Squadron, the unit that delivered a head-on attack on the German formation soon afterwards. One of the Hurricanes collided with a Dornier and both aircraft crashed near Marden. There were no survivors. (Unger)

▲
A Dornier 17 of the 9th Staffel of BG 76 with the unit's emblem and, at the base of the nose, the 20mm cannon carried by these aircraft for low-level attack missions. (Raab)

▶
Hauptmann Joachim Roth, commander of BG 76's 9th Staffel, led the low-altitude attack on Kenley on 18 August. (Raab)

inevitable German fighters.' MacDonell pulled round behind one of the Me 110 escorts and raked it with his fire, and saw it plunge into a steep dive with both engines smoking strongly. Shortly afterwards the Spitfires of No 610 Squadron and Hurricanes of No 615 Squadron joined in the action.

While this was happening, the nine Dorniers of the low-flying attack force had crossed the coast near Beachy Head and were closing on Kenley from the south. The bombers passed over the small market town of Burgess Hill, where people in the streets stood as if glued to the spot and gazed up at the unaccustomed sight of aircraft flying so low. 'At first they did not take us for the enemy, not expecting German aircraft to be flying so low. Then the large crosses on our wings taught them otherwise and in the next instant they were scurrying for cover,' remembered Unteroffizier Guenther Unger, one of the Dornier pilots.

The hedge-hopping Dorniers of the 9th Staffel of BG 76 reached Kenley without interference from the defences, but also without the benefit of surprise: the web of Observer Corps posts had reported each stage of their progress over Sussex and Surrey. Now, as the bombers ran in to attack Kenley, the airfield's defences were manned and ready.

As the raiders pulled up to clear the line of trees at the south side of the airfield, the gunners opened up a withering fire, ' . . . the hail of light flak and machine-gun fire showered around us, the red points of the tracer rounds came flying by. I pushed the aircraft yet lower,' wrote Unger.

Unteroffizier Schumacher, piloting another of the Do 17s, watched the bombs from the leading aircraft ram into the hangars: 'Other bombs were bounding down the runway like rubber balls. Hell was let loose. Then the bombs began their work of destruction. Three hangars collapsed like matchwood. Explosion followed explosion, flames leapt into the sky. It seemed as if my aircraft was grabbed by some giant. Bits of metal and stones clattered against the fuselage; something thudded into my back armour and splinters of glass flew. There was a smell of phosphorus and smouldering cables.'

The low-flying Dorniers delivered a devastatingly accurate attack on Kenley, but in

KENLEY AIRFIELD, AUGUST 1940

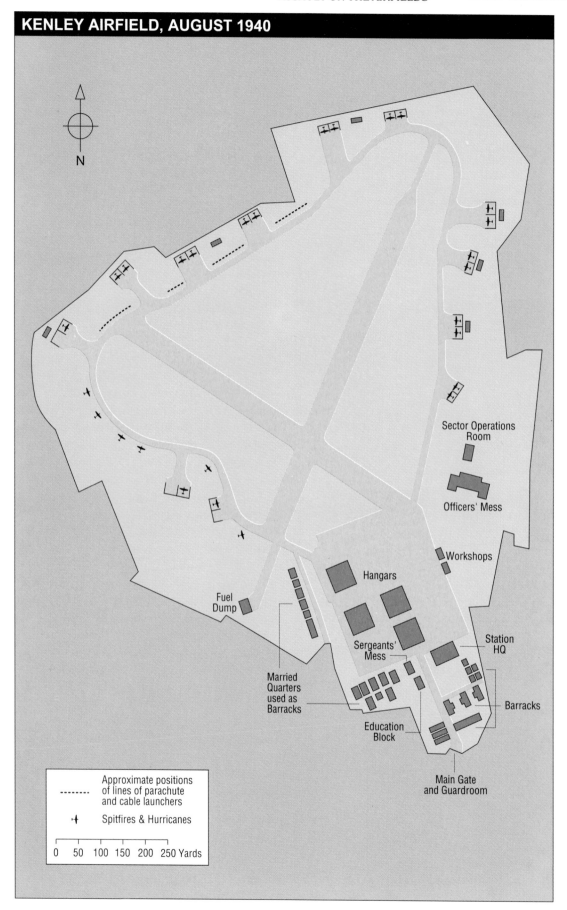

N

Dorniers of the 9th Staffel approaching Beachy Head at low altitude, on their way to attack Kenley.

▶
The early afternoon attack on Kenley and Biggin Hill.
A: 60 Heinkel 111s attacking Biggin Hill.
B: 39 Dornier 17s and Junkers 88s attacking Kenley at high altitude.
C: 9 Dornier 17s making for Kenley at low altitude.

Sector Operations Room

Officers' Mess

Workshops

Hangars

Fuel Dump

Station HQ

Sergeants' Mess

Married Quarters used as Barracks

Barracks

Education Block

Main Gate and Guardroom

- - - - - - - Approximate positions of lines of parachute and cable launchers

✈ Spitfires & Hurricanes

0   50   100 150 200 250 Yards

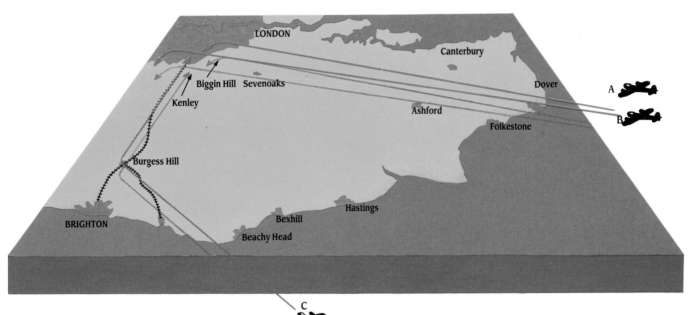

The Parachute and Cable system was designed to counter low-altitude attacks on airfields. The launchers were set out along the perimeter of the airfield at 60ft intervals. As the enemy aircraft approached, the rockets were fired in salvoes of nine or more. At the top of its 600ft trajectory, the rocket released a 480ft-long steel cable that descended by parachute. If an aircraft struck the cable, that released a parachute at the bottom of the wire. The unfortunate machine was left towing the contraption and was likely to go out of control.

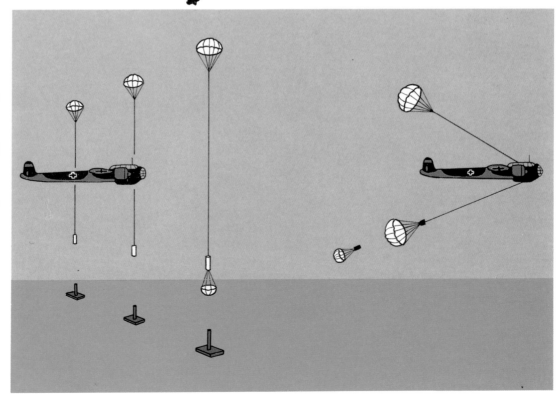

The northern edge of Kenley airfield, pictured during the attack, with cannon shells exploding around a gun position on the ground. The Spitfire in the revetment belonged to No 64 Squadron, and suffered damage during the action.

◀ Hauptmann Joachim Roth's Dornier Do 17 lying burned out in a field not far from Kenley, after being caught by the Parachute and Cable barrage, set on fire by the airfield's ground defences and then being finished off by Hurricanes of No 111 Squadron. All five crewmen suffered wounds and were taken prisoner.

Death of a Bomber. ▶ Dornier 17 of BG 76, hit during the high-level engagement on 18 August by Pilot Officer Alan Eckford of No 32 Squadron, going down with one engine on fire. The aircraft crashed near Oxted.

Oberfeldwebel Wilhelm ▶ Lautersack, the aircraft's flight engineer, baled out and landed with leg injuries. (Lautersack)

▲ Kenley under attack on 18 August, taken from one of the Dorniers in the high-level attack force. The German annotations show: 1 wrecked aircraft, 2 hangar on fire, 2a fire on the north side of the airfield, 3 cratering of the runway.

KENLEY - A TYPICAL FIGHTER AIRFIELD

Situated 13 miles south of the centre of London, during the initial part of the Battle of Britain, Kenley was home for No 64 Squadron with Spitfires and No 615 Squadron with Hurricanes. The fighter base had a complement of 30 officers, 600 airmen and about a hundred airwomen. In addition, to protect the base, there were about a hundred soldiers – anti-aircraft gunners and infantrymen.

Originally Kenley had been a grass airfield, but in 1939 two 800-yard concrete runways had been laid to permit all-weather operations. During the Battle of Britain fighters operated from the runways or the grass, as convenient. A perimeter track nearly a mile and a half long surrounded the landing ground, and jutting from it at irregular intervals ran a dozen lead-offs to the protective revetments for the fighters. Each revetment was surrounded on three sides by an 8ft-high earth-and-brick blast wall, looking from above like a letter 'E' and with room for two fighters. The airfield had sufficient revetments for 24 fighters; other aircraft were dispersed in the open around the airfield.

On the south side of the airfield were four hangars and the administrative buildings. On the eastern edge was the Sector Operations Room whose controllers directed into action the fighters based at Kenley and the nearby airfield at Croydon.

For defence against air attack the airfield was protected by four 40mm Bofors guns, two obsolete 3in guns and a few 0.303in Lewis guns and 20mm Hispano cannon.

doing so they too suffered heavily. One of the bombers was brought down by the airfield's parachute-and-cable defences and crashed immediately beside the airfield. Another Do 17 was hit and set on fire, two more had engines knocked out, and in one the pilot was mortally wounded and the navigator had to take the controls. The four remaining Dorniers had suffered lesser amounts of damage. Then the Hurricanes of No 111 Squadron pounced on the raiders; they immediately finished off the bomber on fire and inflicted further damage on the others.

While the Dorniers were under attack, the high-altitude raiding forces bombed Kenley and Biggin Hill. During their withdrawal, they and their escorts were engaged by six fresh squadrons of Spitfires and Hurricanes and there was a running battle all the way to the coast. When the engagement ended the Luftwaffe had lost twenty-one aircraft destroyed. Fighter Command lost seventeen fighters in air

▶ Damage at Kenley on 18 August.

▶ Smoke from the fires at the airfield, photographed from Coulsdon 2 miles to the north-east. (via Flint)

Wrecked barracks . . . and hangars at Kenley.
▼

▲ Hurricane of No 615 Squadron damaged during the attack. Four of the squadron's aircraft were destroyed on the ground, but such losses were rare. During the entire Battle of Britain less than a score of RAF fighters were destroyed on the ground.

LOW-LEVEL FRACAS OVER SURREY

SOUTH-EAST OF KENLEY, 1.24 PM, 18 AUGUST. As they left Kenley after their destructive low-altitude attack on the airfield, the Dornier 17s of the 9th Staffel of Bomber Geschwader 76 came under attack from Hurricanes of No 111 Squadron. Sergeant Harry Newton sighted one of the low flying bombers and swung into a firing position behind it. The RAF pilot saw tracer rounds coming at him from his intended victim but it looked a puny defence: 'I thought "You've got one gun, I've got eight – you don't stand a chance!" ' Unteroffizier Guenther Unger tried to manoeuvre to avoid the attack, but with one engine knocked out by flak there was little he could do. Newton opened fire and saw his tracers going over the bomber's starboard wing. Then, as he prepared to deliver his *coup de grâce*, Unteroffizier Franz Bergmann manning the rear gun loosed off another burst. Newton recalls: 'I thought "Just a slight correction and I've got him!" But just at that moment he got me, because my cockpit seemed to burst into flames . . . But I was so annoyed at the thought of that Dornier getting away that I put my hand back into the flames, groped for the stick, made my correction and then loosed off a long burst in the direction of where I thought the Dornier was.'

Newton pulled his Hurricane into an almost vertical climb to gain altitude before baling out. During the climb he kept his eyes tightly closed, to protect them from the flames that were burning through the three pairs of gloves he was wearing, and through his flying suit and trousers. As it gained height the fighter's speed fell away rapidly, then the engine coughed to a halt. Newton slammed the stick forwards, kicked himself out of the cockpit and pulled his ripcord. 'At that moment I opened my eyes, in time to see the tail of my Hurricane flash past my right ear, about a foot away. The next thing I knew the parachute had opened and the ground was coming up to meet me.'

The bomber crew watched the blazing Hurricane fall out of the sky and its pilot drop clear. There was no time to gloat over their victim, however, for the Dornier had suffered further damage as a result of Newton's final despairing burst. The German crew reached the Channel, but just short of the French coast their remaining engine lost power and Unger was forced to set the aircraft down on the water. The bomber sank immediately and the crew, unable to inflate their dinghy, had only their life-jackets to support them. After three hours in the water and close to death from exposure, the airmen were rescued by a German Navy patrol boat.

Sergeant Harry Newton of No 111 Squadron with his Hurricane. (Newton)

Low-level fracas over Surrey (continued):
◄
Unteroffizier Guenther Unger. (Unger)
►
Guenther Unger's Dornier Do 17 soon after crossing the coast on 18 August on its final mission. The shadow of his aircraft indicates that it was about 60ft above the ground. In the background is Seaford.

►
Brought together with his former enemies by the author, Harry Newton (centre) shows how he ran in to attack the Dornier to Guenther Unger (left) and Franz Bergmann. (Newton)

combat and five more destroyed on the ground.

Kenley had been hit hard, with three of its four hangars destroyed and the landing ground badly cratered; its fighters had to be diverted to other airfields until some of the craters had been filled in and the unexploded bombs made safe; by the next day, however, the airfield would be operational. Although attacked by 60 bombers, the airfield at Biggin Hill suffered remarkably little damage and was able to continue operating.

Even as the raiders were streaming back to their bases after the first major attack of the day, the forces allocated to the second were airborne and heading for their targets. One hundred and nine Junkers Ju 87 Stukas drawn from Dive Bomber Geschwadern 3 and 77 were making for the airfields at Gosport, Ford and Thorney Island and the radar station at Poling, escorted by more than 150 Me 109s. British radars located the raiders well out to sea, and 68 Spitfires and Hurricanes from five squadrons were scrambled to engage them.

The British squadrons were moving into position to intercept as the vanguard of the raiders crossed the coast. Standing sentry on the esplanade at Bognor, Private Arthur Sindall of the Royal Army Service Corps gazed in awe at the Germans. 'Their immaculate formation, wing-tip to wing-tip, a kind of airborne Trooping the Colour, engendered a grudging admiration. Their black and white crosses were all too clearly visible on the underside of the wings,' he recalled.

Oberleutnant Julius Neumann of Fighter Geschwader 27, flying one of the Me 109 escorts, remembers: 'I saw some small specks emerging from the patchy haze to the north: British fighters! I alerted my Staffel, then swung round to engage.' But the Messerschmitts were too late to prevent the attack by eighteen Hurricanes of Nos 43 and 601 Squadrons. Flight Lieutenant Frank Carey, leading the attack, fired a long burst into one of the Stukas and saw it go down in flames. Pilot Officer Clifford Gray attacked another and saw it begin to belch flames from the underside of the fuselage. Even so the dive-bomber continued on, so he closed to short range and gave it a 5-second burst. There was a bright explosion, then his victim fell into a steep dive and crashed near Nutbourne.

Through the corner of his eye Oberleutnant Johannes Wilhelm glimpsed three or four British fighters come roaring past his Stuka. He

▲
Sergeant Elizabeth Mortimer, an armourer at Biggin Hill, was awarded the Military Medal for helping to make safe unexploded bombs on the airfield. (Mortimer)

▲
Bombs bursting on Biggin Hill airfield, during the attack by Heinkel 111s of BG 1 on 18 August.

had no time to see where they went next, for he was concentrating on holding position in formation and observing the target through the window in the floor of the cabin. In a few seconds he would push the bomber into its

near-vertical attack dive. To one side of Wilhelm a Stuka burst into flames and slid out of the formation, but still he held position. Then came a sudden loud crash from his engine and the aircraft began to shudder. Oil came streaming back over the cabin, blotting out everything outside. More disconcerting still, the cockpit began to fill with smoke: the aircraft was on fire! Wilhelm turned the Stuka on to its back and shouted *'Raus!'* (Get out!) to his gunner. The pilot slid back his canopy and immediately a gout of hot engine oil struck him in the face and almost blinded him. One after the other the two men released their straps and fell clear of the stricken dive-bomber, and their parachutes opened.

As the Stukas dived to attack their targets, the Hurricanes followed. Contrary to what several accounts have implied, a Stuka was almost invulnerable to fighter attack as long as it remained in the dive with its speed controlled by the dive brakes. Frank Carey told the author: 'In the dive they were very difficult to hit, because in a fighter one's speed built up so rapidly that one went screaming past him. But he couldn't dive for ever . . .

Oberleutnant Otto Schmidt had just released his bombs on the airfield at Thorney Island and was pulling out of the dive when something caught his eye to the rear: an enemy fighter, looming large. Then he realized why his gunner had not opened fire – the unfortunate man was collapsed lifeless in his seat. In concentrating on his dive attack, Schmidt had not noticed that his own aircraft had been hit. He pushed his Stuka into a screaming side-slip and the British fighter slid past him.

At her home in Nutbourne, close to the airfield at Thorney Island and right under the Stuka's approach path, housewife Amelia Sopp was sheltering under the stairs eating her lunch. Outside she could hear the screams of diving aircraft, the clatter of machine-gun fire and the bangs of exploding shells and guns. Then her ear caught a different note, that of people shouting. Cautiously she made her way to the kitchen window and peeped outside, then burst out laughing at the incongruous scene that met her eyes. Her next-door neighbour's eight-year-old son was standing on top of the garden shed cheering on the British fighters, while his mother stood beside the

---

'. . . I began to plot the raid approaching Biggin Hill'

Aircraftwoman Elaine Lewis, plotter, Biggin Hill

'When we came on duty the whole operations room was hectic, a mass of activity. Every plotter round the table was marking out raids over Kent and Sussex, and over the Channel en route. The controller and others on the platform were frantically busy in radio contact with our squadrons. I took over a position plotting several raids in Kent and was kept particularly busy keeping up with the information passed to me. Enemy aircraft singly, or in squadrons or even larger numbers, were so numerous.

'I remember the strange feeling as I began to plot the raid approaching Biggin Hill. It came nearer and nearer, until the arrow I placed was immediately over the aerodrome. At the same time we could hear the bombs dropping, falling some distance away. Then as the sounds came nearer the controller yelled for us to take cover. I remember I could see him talking over the R/T to our squadrons while he was sheltering under his desk. There was a huge bang and part of the operations room came crashing down. The glass screen on which we plotted our squadrons was smashed. Shattered glass was everywhere, it was in our hair and cut our stockings but no one was seriously hurt. The table protected us.

'All were strangely silent. Rather shocked, we straggled out over the debris and were told to go to our quarters.'

LUFTWAFFE ATTACK, MID-AFTERNOON 18 AUGUST

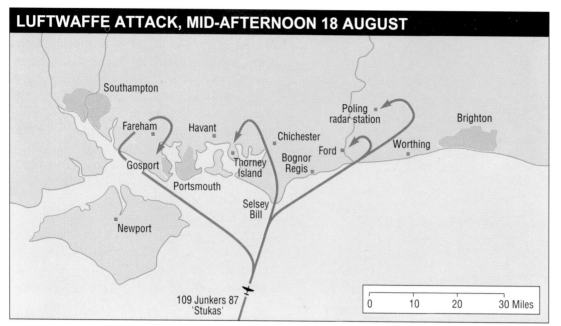

Southampton

Fareham Havant

Gosport

Portsmouth

Newport

Thorney
Island

Chichester

Bognor
Regis

Selsey
Bill

Poling
radar station

Ford

Worthing

Brighton

109 Junkers 87
'Stukas'

0   10   20   30 Miles

The operational life of ▲ Spitfire X4110 was less than twenty-five minutes! Delivered to No 602 Squadron at Westhampnett on the morning of 18 August, there was no time even to paint the squadron letters on the brand-new fighter before Flight Lieutenant Dunlop Urie took it into action over Bognor. Urie came under attack from a Messerschmitt 109, his aircraft was hit and he suffered leg wounds. The pilot landed the aircraft, but its back was broken and it never flew again.

Squadron Leader Derek ▲ Boitel-Gill led the Spitfires of No 152 Squadron in the attack on the dive-bombers along the Bognor-Gosport coast as they came away from their targets.

Leutnant Johannes Wilhelm of Dive Bomber Geschwader 77 was shot down during the attack on Thorney Island and taken prisoner. (Wilhelm) ▶

shed shrieking at him to come down and get into the house. To shield herself from the shell fragments, cartridge cases and spent rounds raining down from above, the woman held her white apron over her head!

As the raiders pulled away from their targets the remaining British squadrons came charging in to engage. The 25-mile-long strip of coastline between Bognor and Gosport became a turmoil of over three hundred aircraft of both sides, twisting and turning to bring guns to bear or to avoid guns being brought to bear.

During this engagement the Luftwaffe lost twenty-four aircraft. Fighter Command lost five. A further twenty British aircraft were destroyed on the ground at Ford and at Gosport, but none of these machines belonged to Fighter Command. The Stukas hit all their targets hard, and the airfield at Ford would be out of action for several weeks.

During the late afternoon the Luftwaffe launched its third major attack of the day: 58 Dornier 17s of Bomber Geschwader 2 and 51 Heinkel 111s of Kampfgeschwader 53 made for the fighter airfields at Hornchurch and North Weald, respectively. Escorting the bombers were 150 Messerschmitts. On the British side, fifteen squadrons of Spitfires and Hurricanes were scrambled to intercept.

As the German formations approached the coast, Nos 32, 54, 56 and 501 Squadrons closed in to engage. Flying Officer Innes West-

macott of No 56, flying a Hurricane, recalls sighting the enemy: 'We had to go up through a bit of cloud and suddenly we saw them and I must say I gulped a bit! It looked an enormous raid.' Squadron Leader 'Minnie' Manton, leading the squadron, split his force into four and ordered three sections to go for the bombers while he and his section moved into position to hold off the Me 110 escorts. Manton succeeded in getting on the tail of one of the escorts and saw his rounds striking home. The Messerschmitt dived away to the south trailing glycol from a punctured radiator.

Meanwhile Innes Westmacott was having trouble from other escorts. To escape them he rolled his Hurricane on its back and pulled it into a vertical dive. The needle of his airspeed indicator edged above 350mph – equivalent to a true airspeed of over 450mph – and so fast that the air rushing past the canopy almost drowned the engine noise. The plane's controls felt as if they had been locked solid. With the sea rushing up to meet him, Westmacott hauled on the stick and almost blacked out, praying that the machine would hold together. It did, and the furious dive shook off his pursuers.

While the other Hurricanes kept the escorts busy, Flying Officer 'Squeak' Weaver of No 56 Squadron was able to get in an attack on one of the bombers. He singled out a Heinkel at the rear of the formation and fired a 10-second burst into it from the rear, then had to break away violently to avoid a Messerschmitt closing on him from behind.

The He 111 that Weaver had hit was flown by Leutnant Walter Leber of Bomber Geschwader 53. From his cockpit Leber saw nothing of the attacker; the first he knew of it was the shout from his gunners that fighters were coming in, then a rattle as they opened up with their machine-guns. The German pilot saw tracers streaking back from the guns of the Heinkels around him. Seconds later the temperature gauge of his starboard engine began to rise rapidly towards the danger mark – the cooling system had been hit. Leber feathered the propeller and shut the engine down. He struggled to keep up with the formation but it was a losing battle, and the Heinkel soon began to drop back. The lone bomber was a sitting duck and it was not long before British fighters took advantage of the fact. Pilot Officer 'John Willie' Hopkin of No 54 Squadron, flying a Spitfire, ran in and fired a long 9-second burst into the bomber, knocking out its other engine and wounding three of the crew. Leber took

his bomber down and made a crash landing on Foulness Island.

As the German formations continued inland, the perfidious British weather intervened to protect the targets more effectively than any man-made defence; a blanket of low cloud, borne in on a north-westerly breeze, concealed the two fighter airfields from the German bomb-aimers. Unable to attack their briefed objectives, the raiders were forced to turn round and head for home.

On the way out there were some sharp actions. Squadron Leader Peter Townsend, leading the thirteen Hurricanes of No 85 Squadron, tried to attack the bombers but found his path blocked by the escorts. He fired at an Me 110 and saw it spiral away. Sergeant John Etherington of No 17 Squadron had cause to remember this part of the engagement. 'It was a proper mix-up. I was going in one direction and the other squadrons came from the opposite direction. I attacked a Messerschmitt 110 and almost collided with a British fighter attacking the same aircraft. Someone

Urie, his feet bandaged, waiting to be taken to hospital after the action. (Urie) ▼

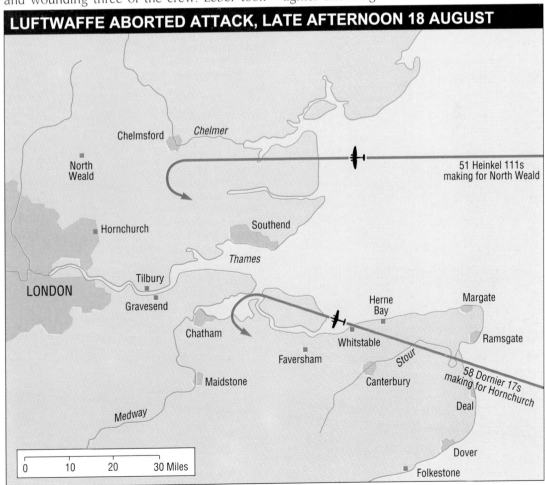

LUFTWAFFE ABORTED ATTACK, LATE AFTERNOON 18 AUGUST

Chelmsford — *Chelmer*

North Weald

Hornchurch

Southend

Thames

Tilbury

LONDON

Gravesend

Chatham

Maidstone

Medway

Faversham

Whitstable

Herne Bay

Canterbury

Stour

Margate

Ramsgate

Deal

Dover

Folkestone

51 Heinkel 111s making for North Weald

58 Dornier 17s making for Hornchurch

0   10   20   30 Miles

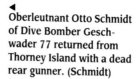

◄
Oberleutnant Otto Schmidt of Dive Bomber Geschwader 77 returned from Thorney Island with a dead rear gunner. (Schmidt)

▲
Hauptmann Herbert Meisel, commander of the Ist Gruppe of Dive Bomber Geschwader 77, killed during the attack on Thorney Island. (Selhorn)

◄ Left and below left: Final moments of a Ju 87 that crashed at West Broyle near Chichester on 18 August. Both members of the crew were killed. (via Sanders)

▼
The spoils of war. RAF personnel pumping petrol from the tank of a Junkers 88 of BG 54 that crash-landed near Tangmere, into a private car belonging to one of them. Such misuse of captured enemy material was illegal, but those in authority usually turned a blind eye. (Lloyd)

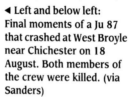

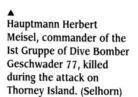

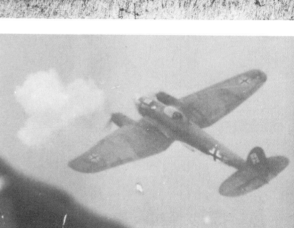

◀
The burning wreck of another Ju 87 which crashed into an orchard near Chidham. (via Sanders)

Lucky to be alive – Unteroffizier Karl Mair, gunner in one of the dive-bombers, was hit by no fewer than eight bullets but suffered only a flesh wound from each. (Selhorn) ▶

The Defiants Leave the Day Battle

Pilot Officer Desmond Hughes, Defiant pilot, No 264 Squadron

'During the week we were at Hornchurch at the end of August we lost five pilots and nine gunners. The squadron commander, the squadron commander designate, and both flight commanders were all killed or wounded.

'By mid-day on the 28th there were only two Defiants serviceable and I flew on the Squadron's last daylight patrol in the Hornchurch Sector. We took off and were being vectored towards thirty-plus enemy aircraft. But before we reached them the controller came up on the radio and said, "I'm terribly sorry, old boy, but they've turned back. Return to base and Pancake." I don't know how the other three felt, but I certainly knew that if the "thirty-plus" had turned out to be Me 109s we would have been in for an interesting time!

'On the next day the half-dozen planes that were made flyable took off from Hornchurch for Kirton-in-Lindsey in Lincolnshire. They were led by a twenty-year-old Pilot Officer, the senior officer on the squadron.'

◀
Fires burning at Royal Naval Air Station Ford, near Chichester, following the destructive attack by dive-bombers.

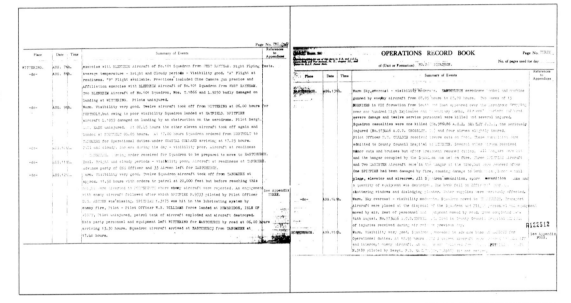

◀
Anti-aircraft shell bursting below a Heinkel 111 of BG 53 on the afternoon of 18 August. (Schierning)

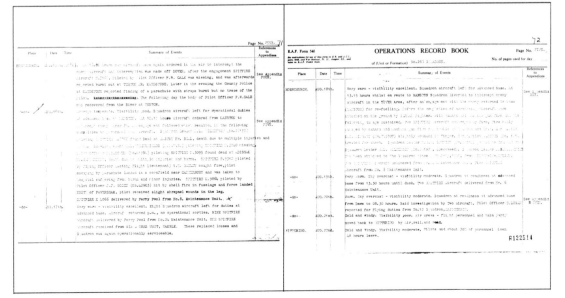

▶
Four pages from the Diary of No 266 Squadron.

'Poor Old Biggin Caught a Packet . . . '

Squadron Leader Michael Crossley, Commander of No 32 Squadron

'Friday, 30 August. Poor old Biggin caught a packet that day. We were sitting at tea in the Mess when the loudspeaker piped up and said "Take cover! Enemy aircraft approaching the aerodrome." We tore to the nearest shelter but nothing happened so presently we forgathered again and went on with tea. Twice more the same thing happened. When it happened a fourth time we got slowly up and strolled outside and watched seven Blenheims flying along in line astern about a mile to the south.

'All of a sudden the leading "Blenheim" did a quick turn to starboard and started a dive at us. We were in the shelter like greased lightning and a few seconds later there was a noise like an express train approaching and WHOOMP – a fourpenny one landed in the road thirty yards away. I really thought my last hour had come . . .

'When all of the Whoomping had finished we came out to see what was what. Several buildings had been hit, and one bomb had landed on a concrete shelter and killed about thirty troops including some WAAF. Most of 79 [Squadron] had an amazing escape. At the time of the warning they were getting into the Humber station wagon to go across to dispersal. They were just passing behind 32's hangar when the WAAF driver perceived what was happening, stopped and told them to go into a shelter which was about 10 yards away. The last of them (there were about ten in the wagon) had just got down inside when a bomb landed alongside the Humber, lifted it bodily seventy feet into the air and dropped it through the roof of our hangar where it landed on the concrete floor upside down.'

◄ Spitfires of No 66 Squadron, and a Hurricane of No 501 Squadron, at Gravesend early in September. (Times Newspapers)

A section of Spitfires of No 66 Squadron taking off from Gravesend. (Times Newspapers) ▼

◀

Hauptmann Horst Tietzen of FG 51, credited with 27 victories, was killed on 18 August when his Bf 109 was shot down by Flight Lieutenant Brothers and Pilot Officer Wlasnowolski of No 32 Squadron. (via Ring)

◀

Pilots of No 65 Squadron at '30 minutes Available' at Rochford during August. (Glaser)

had a go at me – I saw tracer coming past – I did not hang around to find out who it was. I had a couple of bursts at a 109, then it was all over. One moment the air was full of aircraft blazing away at each other and the next the sky was empty, almost like a dream.'

During this engagement the Luftwaffe lost fourteen aircraft and the RAF lost nine.

During the three major attacks and numerous smaller ones on 18 August, the Luftwaffe lost 69 aircraft destroyed or damaged beyond repair. Fighter Command lost 31 fighters destroyed or damaged beyond repair in air combat, and seven destroyed on the ground. A further 29 aircraft were destroyed on the ground, none of them fighters, during the attacks on other airfields.

During that day eleven British fighter pilots were killed and nineteen wounded. Luftwaffe aircrew losses amounted to 94 killed, 25 wounded and 40 taken prisoner. Thus it cost the Luftwaffe nearly two aircraft for each British fighter destroyed, and five Luftwaffe aircrew killed, wounded or taken prisoner for each RAF fighter pilot killed or wounded. The loss of pilots has often been cited as the factor limiting Fighter Command's operations during the battle. But, even allowing for the greater strength of the attacking force, the German losses in trained aircrew were the more serious and damaging. The ratio of the losses between the two sides on 18 August was representative of those during major actions in the Battle of Britain.

Both sides greatly exaggerated the number of enemy aircraft they had destroyed during

THE LUFTWAFFE'S INTELLIGENCE CONUNDRUM

On 17 August the Intelligence Directorate of the Luftwaffe issued its latest assessment of the strength of RAF Fighter Command:

'During the period from 1 July to 15 August 1940 the following enemy aircraft were confirmed destroyed by fighter action, flak and on the ground:

Spitfires	373	Curtisses	9
Hurricanes	180	Defiants	12

'To this figure of 574 enemy fighters destroyed must be added at least 196 due to machines involved in crash-landing, landings damaged beyond repair, accidents, etc, giving a total loss of some 770 enemy fighters. During the same period some 270 to 300 new fighters were built, so the net reduction in enemy fighter strength is estimated at about 470. On 1 July the fighter units had 900 modern fighters so by 16 August there were 430 left; allowing 70 per cent serviceability, there are now 300 combat-ready fighters.

'Unconfirmed but previously reliable reports distribute these combat-ready fighters at present as follows:

South and south-eastern England (south of the line The Wash–Bristol Channel	200
The Midlands	70
Northern England and Scotland	30

The 'Curtisses' mentioned in the report were American-built Curtiss Hawk 75A fighters used in large numbers by the French Air Force and later supplied to Britain; although the type was frequently mentioned in German combat reports during the Battle of Britain, none was operational in the RAF at that time.

Oberst Josef Schmid's Intelligence Directorate had calculated the strength of Fighter Command by the simple expedient of adding the 900 fighters it was thought to possess on 1 July to the 300 new fighters believed to have been delivered from the factories since then, and subtracting the 770 fighters claimed destroyed in action. That gave the strength of Fighter Command as 430 aircraft.

That was the best figure available to the Luftwaffe, but it was wildly removed from the truth. In fact, on 1 July Fighter Command was weaker than the Germans had estimated: its squadrons had 786 modern single-engined fighters on strength, 114 less than thought. But Schmid's calculations underestimated the output from Britain's aircraft factories: during July and the first half of August these had turned out about 720 fighters, more than twice the German estimate. Moreover, during the same period, instead of the German estimate of 770 aircraft lost, Fighter Command had lost 318 Spitfires, Hurricanes and Defiants. That was less than half the Luftwaffe claim. Caught between the hammer of under-estimated production and the anvil of overestimated losses, Schmid's calculation of Fighter Command's numerical strength was wide of the mark. Instead of 430 fighters remaining by the middle of August, Fighter Command's squadrons now possessed more than a thousand Spitfires, Hurricanes and Defiants of which about 850 were serviceable. In addition, there were 300 of these aircraft at storage units ready for immediate issue to units. Thus Fighter Command's day fighter force was about three times stronger than Schmid estimated.

Inexorably the process of defeating Fighter Command continued, on paper at least. By the first week in September Schmid assessed that the force was down to its last fifty fighters and on the point of collapse. The Luftwaffe was about to receive a nasty surprise . . .

the action on 18 August. The Luftwaffe (with 142 enemy aircraft claimed destroyed in the air and on the ground) overclaimed by just over three-to-one. The RAF (with 123 enemy aircraft claimed destroyed by fighters and 15 by anti-aircraft guns) overclaimed by two-to-one.

Following the heavy losses suffered that day, the Junkers 87s took little further part in the Battle. They represented the most effective anti-shipping force available to the Luftwaffe and had to be conserved to counter the Royal Navy when the invasion got under way. Also, following the savage mauling suffered by the 9th Staffel of Bomber Geschwader 76 during its low-level attack on Kenley – four aircraft destroyed and all the other five damaged – the unit made no more low-level attacks.

During this and previous actions the Messerschmitt 110, like the RAF's Defiant, was shown to be extremely vulnerable when confronted by enemy single-seaters. But whereas the Defiant represented a small proportion of Fighter Command's front-line strength, the Me 110 constituted about a quarter of the German fighter force. With the scale of the bomber attacks already being limited by the number of fighters available to escort them, the German High Command was loath to reduce its fighter force still further. It was decided that the Me 110s were to continue to take part in the Battle, although whenever possible they were to receive top cover from Me 109s.

Most far-reaching of the new German measures was Goering's decision that in future a proportion of the escorts was to stick closely to the bombers. Fighters assigned to the close escort of bombers had strict orders that on no account were they to leave the vicinity of their charges; they were to go into action only if the bombers they were protecting came under direct attack from enemy fighters. Ideally there would also be a fighter sweep through the area to break up the British attacks before they could develop, but often this was not the case.

Of course, these decisions on the German side were not immediately known to Fighter Command's leaders, Dowding and Park. They knew only that during the previous eight days' heavy fighting the British squadrons had suffered serious losses. To reduce pilot losses, Air Vice-Marshal Park, commanding No 11 Group, ordered his fighters' controllers that

whenever possible British fighters were to engage the German formations over England rather than over the sea, so that those who baled out would come down on land.

Following the seven days' ferocious fighting up to dusk on the 18th, there were six days when poor weather effectively prevented large-scale air operations. During this lull Dowding decided to give the Defiants another chance: one of the squadrons, No 264, was ordered south to Hornchurch. In an effort to prevent the sort of fighter-versus-fighter combat which had proved so disastrous just over a month earlier, Park instructed his Sector controllers:

'The Defiants whenever practicable are to be detailed to attack the enemy bombers. They may also attack fighters that are attacking ground targets, but are not to be detailed to intercept fighter formations. Moreover the Defiants are not normally to be despatched to intercept raids beyond gliding distance of the coastline except the Thames estuary.'

When the Luftwaffe resumed its attack, on 24 August, there were further heavy raids on the Fighter Command airfields. Thus began a period of nearly two weeks of daily combat during which Fighter Command, and in particular No 11 Group, had to fight for its very existence. On the 24th the airfield at Manston was knocked out of action and had temporarily to be abandoned. On the 26th Kenley, Biggin Hill and Debden were all hit hard. On the 28th, in spite of the controllers' attempts to keep them clear of enemy fighters, the Defiants of No 264 Squadron were caught by Messerschmitt 109s and lost four shot down and three damaged out of twelve aircraft, without shooting down any of the enemy fighters. After that the Defiants were relegated to night operations, for good. On the final day of August there were heavy attacks on Croydon, Hornchurch and Biggin Hill.

September brought no immediate relief for Air Vice-Marshal Park's hard-pressed squadrons. On each of the first six days there were large-scale actions round the fighter airfields; aircraft factories were also hit, although without causing any serious fall in production. In the course of the fighting during the final two weeks of this period, from 24 August to 6 September, Fighter Command had lost 103

▶
Oberleutnant Gerhard Schoepfel shot down four Hurricanes in quick succession on 18 August. He saw action as a fighter pilot throughout the entire war and ended the conflict with a victory score of 40. (Schoepfel)

Pilots of No 501 Squadron at readiness. From left to right, standing: Flying Officer S. Witorzenc, Flight Lieutenant G. Stoney, Sergeant F. Kozlowski; sitting, Sergeant R. Dafforn, Sergeant P. Farnes, Pilot Officer Kenneth Lee, Flight Sergeant J. Gibson and Sergeant H. Adams. Lee and Kozlowski were two of the four pilots shot down by Schoepfel; both were wounded. In other actions that day Dafforn was shot down but baled out uninjured, and Stoney was shot down and killed. (Central Press) ▶

▲
Photographed during a scramble take-off from Rochford on 15 August, these two Hurricanes, P3059 and P3208, were both shot down by Schoepfel three days later. (IWM)

▶
The tail of Schoepfel's Messerschmitt Bf 109, showing the four victory bars denoting his kills on 18 August. (Schoepfel)

pilots killed and 128 wounded. With about 1,500 pilots in his Command, Dowding was losing them at a rate of about one-twelfth per week. During August 250 new pilots emerged from operational training units, but these inexperienced newcomers often fell as easy prey before learning to survive in action.

In the latter half of August the Luftwaffe began to mount night attacks on targets in England, in parallel with those by day. The night raids were far less accurate than those during the day and the raiders scattered their bombs over a wide area. On one of the first of these attacks, on 24 August, a few bombs unintentionally fell on London. That raid would have far-reaching consequences, for it would lead to a retaliatory attack by the RAF on Berlin – the implications of which will be discussed later.

On 25 and 26 August the night raiders hit Birmingham. Then, on the nights of the 28th, 29th, 30th and 31st, Liverpool came under repeated attack from raiding forces of about 150 aircraft. The port came under further attack on the nights of 3, 4 and 5 September.

If the night attacks were far less accurate than those by day, compensating for this was the relative invulnerability of the raiders

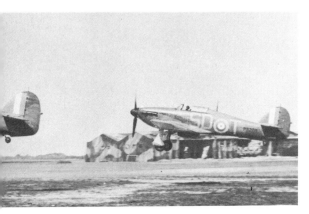

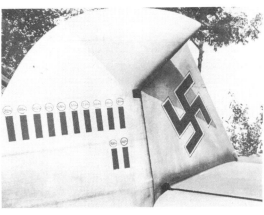

THE ASSAULT ON THE AIRFIELDS – AIRCRAFT LOSSES

	Luftwaffe	RAF	Action
13 August	39	14	Heavy attacks on airfields
14 August	18	9	Heavy attacks on airfields
15 August	79	34	Heavy attacks on airfields
16 August	44	27	Heavy attacks on airfields
17 August	2	1	Little activity
18 August	69	39	Heavy attacks on airfields
19 August	4	5	Poor weather, little activity
20 August	6	1	Poor weather, little activity
21 August	12	4	Poor weather, little activity
22 August	2	4	Poor weather, little activity
23 August	4	1	Poor weather, little activity
24 August	34	18	Day: heavy attacks on airfields Night: some bombs hit London
25 August	19	18	Day: attacks on airfields Night: Birmingham attacked
26 August	38	30	Day: heavy attacks on airfields Night: Birmingham attacked
27 August	9	6	Little activity
28 August	28	13	Day: attacks on airfields Night: Liverpool attacked
29 August	18	10	Day: fighter sweeps Night: Liverpool attacked
30 August	36	24	Day: heavy attacks on airfields Night: Liverpool attacked
31 August	34	38	Day: heavy attacks on airfields Night: Liverpool attacked
1 September	11	13	Day: attacks on airfields Night: Swansea and Bristol hit
2 September	33	14	Day: attacks on airfields
3 September	14	11	Day: attacks on airfields Night: Liverpool attacked
4 September	22	14	Day: attacks on airfields Night: Liverpool attacked
5 September	24	19	Day: attacks on airfields Night: Liverpool attacked
6 September	30	18	Day: attacks on Weybridge and Medway towns Night: London docks hit
TOTALS	629	385	

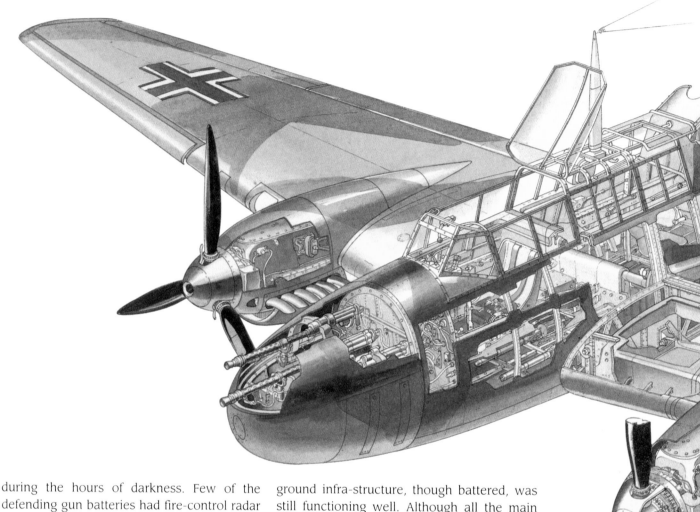

during the hours of darkness. Few of the defending gun batteries had fire-control radar and even fewer RAF fighters carried airborne interception (AI) radar. And in any case these equipments were crude and unreliable, and their operators were learning to handle them from first principles. In contrast to the fierce battles being fought by day, by night it was unusual for a raider to be seen and rare for one to be shot down.

During the opening phase of the Battle the Luftwaffe lost 629 aircraft and the RAF lost 385. This give a loss ratio of 1.6:1 in favour of the RAF, rather less than during the earlier skirmishes but still one satisfactory to the defence.

Fighter Command had taken some hard knocks during this phase of the Battle but its ground infra-structure, though battered, was still functioning well. Although all the main airfields in No 11 Group had suffered damage, there was an efficient organization to fill craters in the landing grounds and only one airfield, that at Manston, was put out of action for more than a few hours. Rarely could raiders catch RAF fighters on the ground: by the time the bombers arrived over an airfield, the fighter squadrons based there were usually airborne and well clear. Fighters able to fly but not fight were sent off on 'survival scrambles,' to keep clear of the enemy and return when the raiders had passed. Aircraft unable to fly were wheeled into the protective revetments or dispersed around the airfield, where they were hard to hit from the air. Despite the almost daily attacks on their airfields over a period of

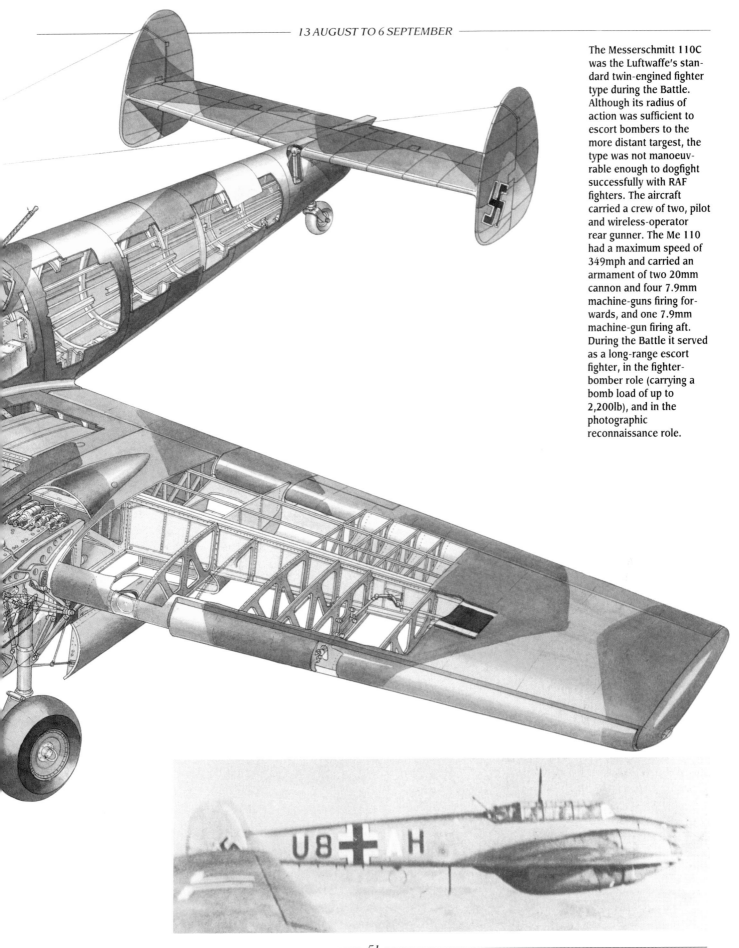

The Messerschmitt 110C was the Luftwaffe's standard twin-engined fighter type during the Battle. Although its radius of action was sufficient to escort bombers to the more distant targest, the type was not manoeuvrable enough to dogfight successfully with RAF fighters. The aircraft carried a crew of two, pilot and wireless-operator rear gunner. The Me 110 had a maximum speed of 349mph and carried an armament of two 20mm cannon and four 7.9mm machine-guns firing forwards, and one 7.9mm machine-gun firing aft. During the Battle it served as a long-range escort fighter, in the fighter-bomber role (carrying a bomb load of up to 2,200lb), and in the photographic reconnaissance role.

LUFTWAFFE UNITS DEPLOYED AGAINST BRITAIN, 7 September 1940

(First figure, aircraft serviceable; second figure, aircraft unserviceable)

AIR FLEET 2, HQ BRUSSELS

LONG-RANGE BOMBERS

Bomber Geschwader 1

Staff Flight	Heinkel 111	5	2	Rosières-en-Santerre
I Gruppe	Heinkel 111	22	14	Montdidier, Clairmont
II Gruppe	Heinkel 111	23	13	Montdidier, Nijmegen
III Gruppe	Junkers 88	–	9	Rosières-en-Santerre

Bomber Geschwader 2

Staff Flight	Dornier 17	6	0	Saint-Leger
I Gruppe	Dornier 17	12	7	Cambrai
II Gruppe	Dornier 17	20	11	Saint-Leger
III Gruppe	Dornier 17	20	10	Cambrai

Bomber Geschwader 3

Staff Flight	Dornier 17	5	1	Le Culot
I Gruppe	Dornier 17	25	4	Le Culot
II Gruppe	Dornier 17	23	4	Antwerp/Deurne
III Gruppe	Dornier 17	19	9	Saint-Trond

Bomber Geschwader 4

Staff Flight	Heinkel 111	5	5	Soesterberg
I Gruppe	Heinkel 111	16	21	Soesterberg
II Gruppe	Heinkel 111	30	7	Eindhoven
III Gruppe	Junkers 88	14	16	Amsterdam/Schiphol

Bomber Geschwader 26

Staff Flight	Heinkel 111	3	3	Gilze-Rijen
I Gruppe	Heinkel 111	7	18	Moerbeke, Courtrai (operated from Wevelghem on 15 September)
II Gruppe	Heinkel 111	7	19	Gilze-Rijen

Bomber Geschwader 30

Staff Flight	Junkers 88	1	–	Brussels
I Gruppe	Junkers 88	1	9	Brussels
II Gruppe	Junkers 88	24	6	Gilze-Rijen

Bomber Geschwader 40

Staff Flight	Focke-Wulf 200	1	1	Bordeaux

Bomber Geschwader 53

Staff Flight	Heinkel 111	3	2	Lille
I Gruppe	Heinkel 111	19	4	Lille
II Gruppe	Heinkel 111	7	22	Lille
III Gruppe	Heinkel 111	4	15	Lille

Bomber Geschwader 76

Staff Flight	Dornier 17	3	3	Cormeilles-en-Vexin
I Gruppe	Dornier 17	19	7	Beauvais/Tille
II Gruppe	Junkers 88	21	6	Creil
III Gruppe	Dornier 17	17	7	Cormeilles-en-Vexin

Bomber Geschwader 77

Staff Flight	Junkers 88	1	–	Laon
I Gruppe	Junkers 88	31	5	Laon
II Gruppe	Junkers 88	25	7	Asch
III Gruppe	Junkers 88	19	11	Laon

Bomber Gruppe 126

	Heinkel 111	26	7	Marx

DIVE-BOMBERS AND FIGHTER-BOMBERS

Dive Bomber Geschwader 1

Staff Flight	Ju 87, Do 17	5	2	Saint-Pol
II Gruppe	Junkers 87	29	14	Pas de Calais

Dive Bomber Geschwader 2

Staff Flight	Ju 87, Do 17	9	2	Tramecourt
II Gruppe	Junkers 87	22	5	Saint-Omer, Saint-Trond

Lehrgeschwader 1 (Tactical Development Geschwader)

IV Gruppe	Junkers 87	28	14	Tramecourt

Lehrgeschwader 2 (fighter-bomber unit)

II Gruppe	Me 109	27	5	Saint-Omer

SINGLE-ENGINED FIGHTERS

Fighter Geschwader 1

Staff Flight	Me 109	3	1	Pas de Calais area

Fighter Geschwader 3

Staff Flight	Me 109	3	–	Samer
I Gruppe	Me 109	14	9	Samer
II Gruppe	Me 109	21	3	Samer
III Gruppe	Me 109	23	2	Desvres

Fighter Geschwader 26

Staff Flight	Me 109	3	1	Audembert
I Gruppe	Me 109	20	7	Audembert
II Gruppe	Me 109	28	4	Marquise
III Gruppe	Me 109	26	3	Caffiers

Fighter Geschwader 27

Staff Flight	Me 109	4	1	Etaples
I Gruppe	Me 109	27	6	Etaples
II Gruppe	Me 109	33	4	Montreuil
III Gruppe	Me 109	27	4	Sempy

Fighter Geschwader 51

Staff Flight	Me 109	4	1	Saint-Omer
I Gruppe	Me 109	33	3	Saint-Omer, Saint-Inglevert
II Gruppe	Me 109	13	9	Saint-Omer, Saint-Inglevert
III Gruppe	Me 109	31	13	Saint-Omer

Fighter Geschwader 52

Staff Flight	Me 109	1	1	Laon/Couvron
I Gruppe	Me 109	17	4	Laon/Courvon
II Gruppe	Me 109	23	5	Pas de Calais area
III Gruppe	Me 109	16	15	Pas de Calais area

Fighter Geschwader 53

Staff Flight	Me 109	2	–	Pas de Calais area
II Gruppe	Me 109	24	9	Wissant
III Gruppe	Me 109	22	8	Pas de Calais area

Fighter Geschwader 54

Staff Flight	Me 109	2	2	Holland
I Gruppe	Me 109	23	5	Holland
II Gruppe	Me 109	27	8	Holland
III Gruppe	Me 109	23	5	Holland

Fighter Geschwader 77

I Gruppe	Me 109	40	2	Pas de Calais area

TWIN-ENGINED FIGHTERS

Destroyer Geschwader 2 (Destroyer Geschwader 2)

Staff Flight	Me 110	–	1	Pas de Calais area
I Gruppe	Me 110	10	10	Amiens, Caen
II Gruppe	Me 110	10	18	Guyancourt/Caudran

Destroyer Geschwader 26

Staff Flight	Me 110	3	–	Lille
I Gruppe	Me 110	14	19	Abbeville, Saint-Omer
II Gruppe	Me 110	17	8	Crécy
III Gruppe	Me 110	17	8	Barley, Arques

Lehrgeschwader 1

V Gruppe	Me 110	19	4	Ligescourt, Alencon

Erprobungsgruppe 210 (fighter-bomber unit)

	Me 109, Me 110	17	9	Denain

LONG-RANGE RECONNAISSANCE
Reconnaissance Gruppe 22

1 Staffel	Do 17, Me 110	9	4	Lille

Reconnaissance Gruppe 122

1 Staffel	Junkers 88	3	5	Holland
2 Staffel	Ju 88, He 111	9	1	Brussels/Melsbroek
3 Staffel	Ju 88, He 111	10	1	Eindhoven
4 Staffel	Ju 88, He 111, Me 110	9	4	Brussels
5 Staffel	Ju 88, He 111	11	–	Haute-Fontain

MARITIME RECONNAISSANCE AND MINELAYING AIRCRAFT
Coastal Patrol Gruppe 106

1 Staffel	Heinkel 115	4	6	Brittany area
2 Staffel	Dornier 18	6	3	Brittany area
3 Staffel	Heinkel 115	6	3	Borkum

AIR FLEET 3, HQ PARIS

LONG-RANGE BOMBERS
Lehrgeschwader 1

Staff Flight	Junkers 88	3	–	Orléans/Bricy
I Gruppe	Junkers 88	13	14	Orléans/Bricy
II Gruppe	Junkers 88	19	12	Orléans/Bricy
III Gruppe	Junkers 88	19	11	Chateaudun

Bomber Geschwader 27

Staff Flight	Heinkel 111	4	3	Tours
I Gruppe	Heinkel 111	13	22	Tours
II Gruppe	Heinkel 111	15	17	Dinard, Bourges
III Gruppe	Heinkel 111	13	7	Rennes

Bomber Geschwader 40

I Gruppe	Focke-Wulf 200	4	3	Bordeaux

Bomber Geschwader 51

Staff Flight	Junkers 88	–	1	Orly
I Gruppe	Junkers 88	13	20	Melun
II Gruppe	Junkers 88	17	17	Orly
III Gruppe	Junkers 88	27	7	Etampes

Bomber Geschwader 54

Staff Flight	Junkers 88	–	1	Evreux
I Gruppe	Junkers 88	18	12	Evreux
II Gruppe	Junkers 88	14	12	St André

Bomber Geschwader 55

Staff Flight	Heinkel 111	6	–	Villacoublay
I Gruppe	Heinkel 111	20	7	Dreux
II Gruppe	Heinkel 111	22	8	Chartres
III Gruppe	Heinkel 111	20	5	Villacoublay

Bomber Gruppe 100

	Heinkel 111	7	21	Vannes

Bomber Gruppe 606

	Dornier 17	29	4	Brest, Cherbourg

Bomber Gruppe 806

	Junkers 88	18	9	Nantes, Caen

DIVE-BOMBERS
Dive Bomber Geschwader 3

Staff Flight	Do 17, He 111	6	1	Brittany area
I Gruppe	Junkers 87	34	3	Brittany area

SINGLE-ENGINED FIGHTERS
Fighter Geschwader 2

Staff Flight	Me 109	2	3	Beaumont-le-Roger
I Gruppe	Me 109	24	5	Beaumont-le-Roger
II Gruppe	Me 109	18	4	Beaumont-le-Roger
III Gruppe	Me 109	19	11	Le Havre

Fighter Geschwader 53

I Gruppe	Me 109	27	7	Brittany area

TWIN-ENGINED FIGHTERS
Destroyer Geschwader 76

Staff Flight	Me 110	2	2	
II Gruppe	Me 110	12	15	Le Mans, Abbeville
III Gruppe	Me 110	8	11	Laval

LONG-RANGE RECONNAISSANCE
Lehrgeschwader 2

7 Staffel	Me 110	9	5	

Reconnaissance Gruppe 14

4 Staffel	Me 110, Do 17	9	3	Normandy area

Reconnaissance Gruppe 31

3 Staffel	Me 110, Do 17	5	4	St Brieuc

Reconnaissance Gruppe 121

3 Staffel	Ju 88, He 111	6	4	North-West France
4 Staffel	Ju 88, Do 17	5	8	Normandy

Reconnaissance Gruppe 123

1 Staffel	Ju 88, Do 17	7	3	Paris area
2 Staffel	Ju 88, Do 17	8	2	Paris area
3 Staffel	Ju 88, Do 17	9	3	Buc

AIR FLEET 5, HQ KRISTIANSUND, NORWAY

SINGLE-ENGINED FIGHTERS
Fighter Geschwader 77

II Gruppe	Me 109	35	9	Southern Norway

LONG-RANGE RECONNAISSANCE
Reconnaissance Gruppe 22

2 Staffel	Dornier 17	5	4	Stavanger
3 Staffel	Dornier 17	5	4	Stavanger

Reconnaissance Gruppe 120

1 Staffel	He 111, Ju 88	2	11	Stavanger

Reconnaissance Gruppe 121

1 Staffel	He 111, Ju 88	2	5	Stavanger, Aalborg

MARITIME RECONNAISSANCE AND MINELAYING AIRCRAFT
Coastal Patrol Gruppe 506

1 Staffel	Heinkel 115	6	2	Stavanger
2 Staffel	Heinkel 115	5	3	Trondheim, Tromsö
3 Staffel	Heinkel 115	6	2	List

Air Fleet	2	3	5	Total
Single-engined Fighters	533	90	35	658
Twin-engined Fighters	107	22	–	129
Single-engined Bombers	120	34	–	154
Twin-engined Bombers	484	310	–	794
Four-engined Bombers	–	4	–	4
Reconnaissance	51	58	14	123
Coastal aircraft	16	–	17	33
TOTAL	1,311	518	66	1,895

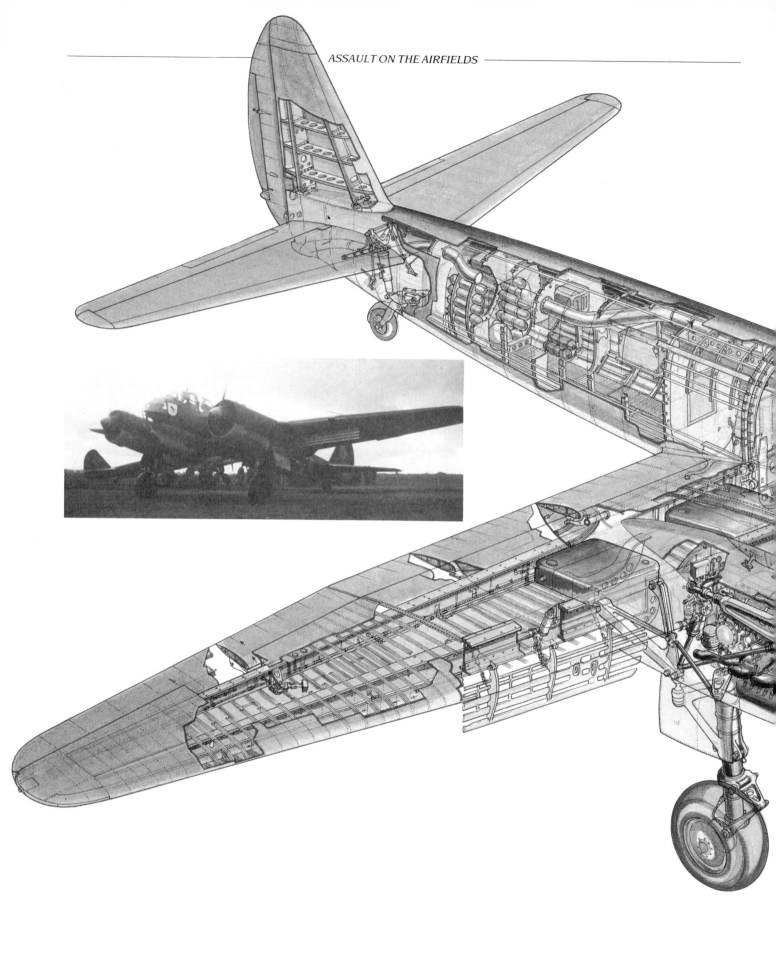

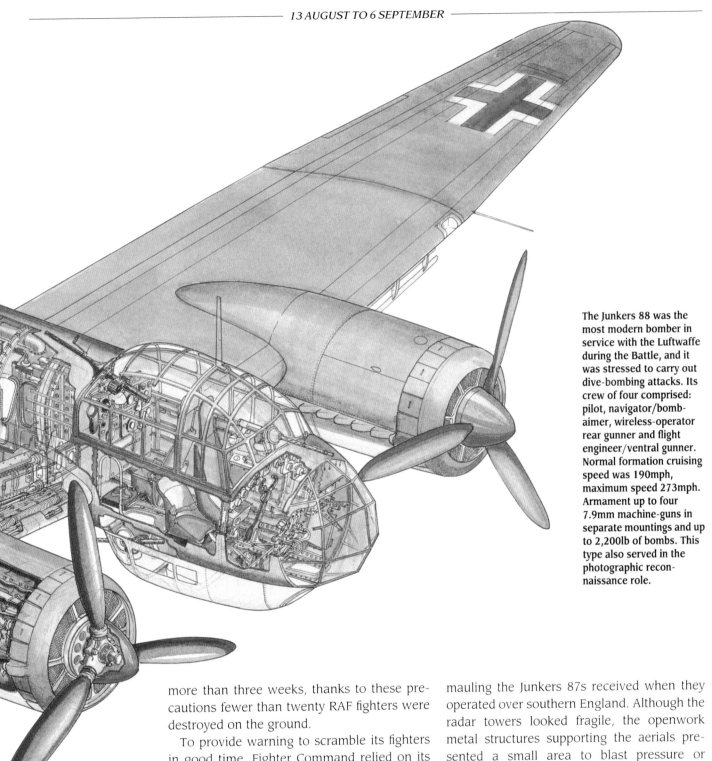

The Junkers 88 was the most modern bomber in service with the Luftwaffe during the Battle, and it was stressed to carry out dive-bombing attacks. Its crew of four comprised: pilot, navigator/bomb-aimer, wireless-operator rear gunner and flight engineer/ventral gunner. Normal formation cruising speed was 190mph, maximum speed 273mph. Armament up to four 7.9mm machine-guns in separate mountings and up to 2,200lb of bombs. This type also served in the photographic recon-naissance role.

more than three weeks, thanks to these pre-cautions fewer than twenty RAF fighters were destroyed on the ground.

To provide warning to scramble its fighters in good time, Fighter Command relied on its coastal radar stations. The radars were attacked from the air, but they also proved difficult targets. From above, the radar stations represented very small pinpoint targets. The buildings containing their vital equipment were protected by revetments, and were im-pervious to anything but a direct hit. Only dive-bombing gave the accuracy necessary to hit such small targets, and we have seen the mauling the Junkers 87s received when they operated over southern England. Although the radar towers looked fragile, the openwork metal structures supporting the aerials pre-sented a small area to blast pressure or fragmentation effects and few were knocked down. Despite several attacks on radar sta-tions, only one was put out of action for more than a few hours.

From the Luftwaffe point of view, however, it looked as if Fighter Command was on its last legs. Now, it seemed, was the time for a bold lunge at Britain's heart, to end her defiance for once and for all.

3. THE ATTACK ON LONDON
7 September to 1 October

'In approaching the prospects for a successful air campaign . . . [against Great Britain] there is one conspicuously favourable factor which will tend to influence Germany's judgment and encourage her to hope for success, and that is the exposed position and vulnerability of London . . . Nothing that either France or ourselves can attack in Germany can have quite the immediate and decisive results that Germany may hope to gain by an overwhelming attack on London.'
Marshal of the Royal Air Force Sir Edward Ellington, Chief of Air Staff, speaking before the war

DURING THE FINAL WEEK in August the Royal Air Force had begun attacking targets in Germany, notably Berlin, in retaliation for the stray bombs that had fallen on London. The move enraged Hitler, who ordered a series of heavy attacks on the British capital as a reprisal.

The new phase in the bombardment began on 7 September. The morning and early afternoon were quiet, with only reconnaissance activity over southern England. It was a fine sunny day and that, in contrast with the intensive action of the previous two weeks, made the silence yet more ominous. The uneasy calm ended shortly before 4 pm when the radar stations began passing plots on yet another large-scale attack building up over the Pas de Calais. The raiding force crossed the coast at 4.16 pm: some 350 bombers, escorted by more than 600 fighters, forming a huge phalanx of aircraft advancing relentlessly across Kent.

No 11 Group's controllers scrambled almost every available squadron but, ignorant of the raiders' objective, they deployed the fighters to meet yet another attack on airfields. Only four squadrons were in position to block an attack on London, and the powerful force of escorts brushed these aside with little difficulty.

When they reached the capital the bombers delivered a devastating attack on the dockland area to the east of the city, starting fierce fires among the rows of warehouses. Soon, some of these fires were blazing out of control.

During its first pitched battle over and around the capital, Fighter Command did not really get to grips with the enemy. The Luftwaffe lost 40 aircraft, while the RAF lost 21 fighters destroyed and an unusually heavy loss of pilots – seventeen killed or seriously wounded.

The Fire-Fighters

Front Line, the Official Story of Civil Defence

'On 7 September we took our pumps to East India Dock, to Rum Wharf. The first line of warehouses was ablaze from end to end . . . Most of us had the wind up to start with. It was all new, but we were all unwilling to show fear however much we might feel it. You looked around and saw the rest doing their job. You couldn't let them down, you just had to get on with it. You began to make feeble jokes to each other and gradually you got accustomed to it . . . The fires had a stunning effect. Wherever the eye could see, vast sheets of flame and a terrific roar. It was so bright that there was no need for headlights.

'The fire was so huge that we could do little more than make a feeble attempt to put it out. The whole of that warehouse was a raging inferno, against which were silhouetted groups of pygmy firemen directing their futile jets at the wall of flame . . .

'Occasionally we would glance up and then we would see a strange sight. For a flock of pigeons kept circling round overhead almost all night. They seemed lost, as if they couldn't understand the unnatural dawn. It looked like sunrise all round us. The pigeons seemed white in the glare, birds of peace making a strange contrast with the scene below.

'When the real dawn came at about five, the Germans eased off their blitz. The All-Clear raised a weary cheer. By 7 o'clock I was hunched half-asleep across the branch holder. At last the relief crews arrived. Knowing that we were returning home gave us that extra ounce of strength without which we could hardly have hoisted the rolled-up lengths on our shoulders.'

London Burning, 7 September

Wing Commander John Hodsoll, Inspector General of Air Raid Precautions, who watched the 7 September raid from the roof of the Home Office building in Whitehall

'It was indeed an awe-inspiring sight that met our eyes. A huge cloud of black smoke was billowing and spiralling up into the clear blue sky; great spurts of flame were shooting up; there was a dull thud of bombs as they exploded and reverberated in the distance, and an acrid smell of burning was borne in on the wind. The docks looked as if they had been reduced to one great inferno. Above it all, just visible, was a maze of tiny dots with their white tails of vapour, high up in the sky; and here and there the signs of combat, of weaving trails, as our fighters did their best to parry this thrust at the heart of London. The spectacle had an almost eerie fascination, which held us spellbound and immobile, and it was some little time before I could drag myself away and descend into the street. There, too, I found a strange air of unreality. The streets were nearly empty, since the warning had gone; but there were streams of fire engines and appliances speeding to the docks, with fire bells ringing and echoing their message of urgency. Wardens were controlling what other traffic there was, and the few pedestrians in sight seemed dazed now the long-awaited blow had fallen.'

▲ **Smoke rising from the fires in the dockland area of London on the afternoon of 7 September, seen from the roof of one of the buildings overlooking Fleet Street.**

◀ **The huge fire blazing at the Surrey Docks on the night of 7–8 September required 130 fire pumps to bring it under control.**

A sombre-looking Winston Churchill, pictured with the Town Clerk of West Ham, Charles Cranfield, inspects the gutted works of the Silvertown Rubber Company at Winchester Street on 8 September. (IWM) ▶

After dark more than 300 bombers returned to the city and delivered a further powerful attack on the docklands. The raid was to set the pattern for the nights to follow. With little to fear from the defences, the bombers flew direct routes from their bases, converging on London from every direction between south-west to due east. The bombers arrived over the capital in ones and twos and the bombing continued for more than six hours, from 10.10 pm until 4.30 am the following morning.

With their target clearly marked by the fires started during the daylight attack, the night raiders dropped their loads of high-explosive and incendiary bombs to reinforce these and disrupt the work of the fire-fighters. By 1 am there were nine fires that had grown so large that they merited the official description 'conflagration'. One of these, in the area around Quebec Yard of the Surrey Docks, continued spreading and grew into the fiercest single fire ever recorded in Britain. (In this context a 'conflagration' was defined as 'a major fire that was spreading and requiring more than one hundred pumps to bring it under control'; a 'major fire' was one that required more than thirty pumps, while a 'serious fire' required between eleven and thirty pumps to bring it under control.)

When the all-clear sounded on the morning of 8 September it was recorded that, in addition to the nine conflagrations, there had been nineteen major fires, forty serious fires and nearly a thousand smaller fires. Casualties had been heavy: 430 killed and about 1,600 seriously injured.

London's fire brigades spent the daylight hours of the 8th in a desperate battle, for any fires that remained would serve as beacons to guide the German bombers back to the capital that night. In spite of Herculean efforts, several of the fires resisted all attempts to extinguish them and there was light aplenty to guide in the 200 bombers that returned to the city after darkness fell. The fires that had survived were fed afresh and several new ones were started; by the morning of the 9th twelve full conflagrations were raging. A further 412 people had been killed and 747 were seriously injured. The bombers would be back in force on the following night and, with one exception due to bad weather, on every one of the sixty-five nights that followed. The great 'Night Blitz' had begun.

During the second daylight attack on the city, on the afternoon of the 9th, cloud prevented accurate bombing. Twenty-five German aircraft were destroyed for a loss of eighteen British fighters. Two days later, on the 11th, the Luftwaffe returned to the city and added further damage to the dock areas. Fighter Command emerged from that action the loser – in shooting down 24 German aircraft, it lost 28 Spitfires and Hurricanes. Three days later, on the 14th, German bombers attempted a further attack on the capital, only to be defeated yet again by cloud over the targets. On that day the Luftwaffe lost ten aircraft and Fighter Command twelve.

During the first four daylight attacks on London, for one reason or another the British fighter controllers had failed to bring a major proportion of their force into action. On the initial attack, the shift against the capital had come as a surprise and the fighters had been positioned to block yet another raid on airfields. During the next three attacks the cloud that hindered accurate bombing had also hindered the tracking of the German formations by ground observers, making it difficult to vector the fighter squadrons on to the raiders. This unconnected series of failures would lead the German High Command to an entirely erroneous assessment of the way the battle was progressing.

During the first four daylight raids on London, Luftwaffe officers noted that the bombers had not been engaged with the ferocity and effectiveness that had characterized many of the August actions. It seemed that Fighter Command might indeed be on the point of collapse, long predicted in the German calculations, and required only a couple more large-scale actions to finish it off as an effective fighting force. If the assessment were correct and Fighter Command really was at its last gasp, the correct strategy was to send a series of large attacks against the capital, to draw the remaining British fighters into action to suffer further losses at the hands of the escorting Messerschmitts.

To this end, for 15 September the Luftwaffe planned to mount the heaviest blow of all against the British capital: two separate

A Night Raider Remembers

Unteroffizier Horst Goetz, Heinkel 111 pilot, Bomber Geschwader 100

'I have no particular memories of individual operations. They were all quite routine, like running a bus service. The London flak defences put on a great show – at night the exploding shells gave the place the appearance of bubbling pea soup. But very few of our aircraft were hit – I myself never picked up so much as a shell fragment. On rare occasions one of my crew might catch sight of a British night fighter, but it seems they never saw us and we were never attacked. During our return flights the radio-operator would often tune in his receiver to a music programme, to provide some relief from the monotony.'

◄ During a fight with Messerschmitts on 9 September Pilot Officer Alan Wright of No 92 Squadron had a 7.9mm round hit his cockpit from behind. The bullet passed through the perspex hood, nicked the windscreen frame near the top, bounced off the inside of the laminated glass windscreen and smashed the reflector gunsight. Wright was not injured. (Wright)

◄ The attacks on London called for the escorting Messerschmitt 109s to operate at the limit of their radius of action, and several were lost when they ran out of fuel on the way home. This one just made it back to the coast of France.

◄ Smoke plumes mark the pyres of two Heinkel 111s of BG 1, shot down within a few hundred yards of each other near Lydd on 11 September.

Warehouses burning at St Katherine's Dock, on the night of 11 September. (IWM) ▼

attacks, one against a nodal point in the rail system and the other against the docks, with a couple of hours between each. Every available Messerschmitt 109 unit in Air Fleet 2 was to take part in the escort of the attacks, with many of the fighters flying double sorties.

If successful, the attacks planned for the 15th would knock out a focal point in the rail network, they would destroy quantities of supplies imported from overseas, they would strike at civilian morale by demonstrating London's vulnerability to attack and lastly, and most important of all, they would impose a further drain on the RAF's dwindling fighter strength.

The first of the day's attacks on London was planned to open shortly before noon. The raiding force comprised 21 Messerschmitt 109 fighter-bombers of Lehrgeschwader 2 and 27 Dornier 17s of Bomber Geschwader 76, escorted by about 180 Me 109s. The fighter-bombers were to carry out diversionary attacks on railway targets in the south-eastern quarter of the city, then the Dorniers were to bomb rail viaducts and the conglomeration of lines running through Battersea.

Almost from the start the operation went wrong. As the Dorniers were climbing towards the Pas de Calais to link up with their fighter escort, they ran into a layer of cloud that was thicker than expected. The bombers were forced to break formation and their leader, Major Alois Lindemayr, had to orbit above cloud for about ten minutes to reassemble his force. The bombers reached the Pas de Calais and picked up their escorts, then headed north-west for London. And again the weather took a hand in the proceedings, this time in the

shape of a 90mph headwind at the bombers' altitude of 16,000 feet.

The Me 109 fighter-bombers reached the capital as planned and delivered their attack. They scattered their bombs across the boroughs of Lambeth, Streatham, Dulwich and Penge, causing little damage and few casualties, then withdrew without loss.

Meanwhile the Dornier 17s and their escorting Messerschmitts fought their way across the length of Kent in a series of skirmishes with eleven squadrons of Spitfires and Hurricanes. Due to the energetic handling of the escorts, the bombers reached the outskirts of London with their formation intact and without the loss of a single aircraft. Now, however, the delays incurred in reforming the formation over France and battling through the headwind had their inevitable effect. The force reached the target area more than half an hour behind schedule. For the Dorniers it was not serious, they had a large enough fuel reserve. But for the Me 109s it was another matter; even under optimum conditions London lay at the limit of their radius of action. When they reached the outskirts of the capital the German fighter units were low on fuel, and one by one they had to break away and turn for home. By the time the Dorniers entered their bombing runs for the attack on Battersea there were virtually no escorts left.

Ignorant of the Germans' predicament, Air Vice-Marshal Park had already decided to fight his main action over the capital. To that end no fewer than twelve squadrons of Spitfires and Hurricanes were converging on the city from all directions. Most of the fighter squadrons flew in pairs, but from Duxford near Cambridge came the five squadrons of Squadron Leader Douglas Bader's 'Big Wing,' going into action for the first time at full strength.

The German bombers held tight formation and traded blows with their tormentors, but then one of their number suffered engine damage and was forced to drop back. The straggler immediately came under attack from several fighters; it was badly shot up and three of the crew baled out. When the formation turned for home after releasing its bombs, the lone Dornier continued doggedly on its north-westerly heading over the capital and still under attack from British fighters. Sergeant

Ray Holmes of No 504 Squadron ran in to attack the bomber from head-on, but shortly after he opened fire his Hurricane's guns fell silent – he was out of ammunition. Holmes later recalled, 'There was no time to weigh up the situation. His aeroplane looked so flimsy, I did not think of it as something solid and substantial . . . I thought my plane would cut right through it, not allowing for the fact that his plane was as strong as mine.'

A split second later the fighter's port wing struck the port fin of the Dornier, shearing off the entire tail. Deprived of the stability provided by that vital appendage, the bomber's nose dropped violently. That imposed enormous forces on the upper surface of the wing, and on each side the outer wing snapped off as if it had been made from balsa wood and tissue paper. The Hurricane had suffered severe structural damage also, and it too was falling out of control. Holmes jumped clear.

The Dornier entered a violent spin, still carrying its full complement of bombs. The savage G forces caused further failures of the plane's already weakened structure and two 110-pounders and a container of incendiary bombs wrenched themselves off their mountings and smashed out through the side of the bomb bay. One 110-pounder plunged into the roof of Buckingham Palace and passed through a couple of floors before it came to rest in the bathroom of one of the royal apartments. The other 110-pounder, and the container with sixteen incendiary bombs, landed in the Palace grounds. The fuses of the two larger bombs had not been made 'live' and neither detonated. Some of the incendiary bombs ignited on hitting the ground, starting small grass fires, but these were immediately extinguished by members of the fire-watching team at the Palace. No member of the Royal Family was in residence at the time.

Holmes' Hurricane plummeted into the junction of Buckingham Palace Road and Pimlico Road, Chelsea. The fighter's engine, weighing about half a ton, smashed through the tarmac and rammed deep into the soil beneath, demolishing a water main on the way. The main section of the Dornier came down beside a jeweller's shop in the forecourt of Victoria Station; the severed tail unit landed on the roof of a house in Vauxhall Bridge Road. One of the

bomber's outer wing sections, borne on the strong north-easterly wind, fluttered for a mile before it finally came to earth south of the Thames in Newburn Street, Vauxhall.

Remarkably, considering that the bombs and wreckage of both aircraft fell on a built-up area, there were no injuries on the ground. Ray Holmes came down on the roof of a three-storey block of flats in Pimlico and his parachute immediately deflated. The Hurricane pilot would probably have been killed or seriously injured falling off the roof, had his parachute not snagged on an up-spout and arrested his descent at the last moment.

Of the three German crewmen who baled out of the Dornier before it was rammed, two were taken into captivity soon after landing. The third man was less fortunate. He came down near the Oval underground station in Kennington and was immediately set upon by civilians. Before soldiers could rescue him he was badly beaten up, and he died of his injuries soon afterwards.

As it left the city the main formation of Dorniers was under heavy attack from more than a dozen squadrons of fighters. One of the bombers, that piloted by Feldwebel Rolf Heitsch, carried an experimental flame-thrower installation intended for use against enemy fighters. One of Heitsch's engines was knocked out and he dived for the safety of a bank of cloud, followed by several fighters. As each ran in to attack, the bomber's radio-operator loosed off a burst of flame, but the weapon was a complete failure; the oil fuel failed to burn properly in the rarefied air at high altitude and produced a thin plume of flame only about a hundred yards long. Far from scaring off the attackers, the sight of the flames strengthened their resolve – to the RAF pilots it appeared that the Dornier was about to catch fire. Heitsch's other engine was knocked out, and he crash-landed the near Sevenoaks.

During the action eight other bombers were forced out of formation, and four of them were finished off by fighters shortly afterwards.

Near Maidstone the Me 109s assigned to cover the Dorniers' withdrawal linked up with their charges and shepherded the survivors home, assisted by the same 90mph wind that had impeded the raiders on their way in. Of the twenty-five bombers that had crossed the

▶ Feldwebel Horst Goetz of Bomber Gruppe 100 with his Heinkel He 111. (Goetz)

'Like bubbling pea soup . . . ' was how Goetz remembered the scene over London during the night raids. The points of light are from fires burning on the ground and exploding anti-aircraft shells. (via Dierich)
▼

▶ Page from Logbook of Pilot Officer Arthur Vokes, a Spitfire pilot of No 19 Squadron, describing his part in the action on 15 September.

The Heinkel 100 was built in competition with the Messerschmitt 109. Although it was faster, the Heinkel was more difficult to handle and the type was not ordered into production for the Luftwaffe. In mid-1940, as a deliberate act of deception, nine of the twelve He 100Ds built were painted in spurious unit markings and lined up for propaganda photos intended to show the fighter, redesignated as the 'Heinkel 113', in operational service.

The He 113 appeared in all British recognition manuals of the early war period, and RAF pilots reported frequent combats with them during the Battle of Britain. This combat report, written on 15 September by Pilot Officer

L. Stevens of No 17 Squadron, was one of several that mentioned the non-existent German fighter. Without doubt the fighters that attacked Stevens had been Messerschmitt 109s.

Propaganda photo of a victory bar being painted on the tail of an 'He 113'. In fact this fighter never fired its guns in anger. (via Schliephake)

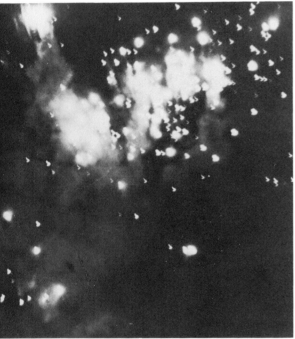

MORNING ACTION

OFF SALCOMBE, 8.45 AM, 15 SEPTEMBER. Flying Officer Dennis David and Pilot Officer Trevor Jay of No 87 Squadron intercept a Heinkel 111 of Weather Reconnaissance Staffel 51 off the Devon coast. 'It was a funny sort of day, with layers of cloud both above and below the Heinkel,' David later recalled. 'It seemed the pilot was experienced, when he saw us he turned south trying to get away. He was trying to get back into cloud. But we had plenty of speed, we were on him before he could get there.' Closing fast, David swung behind the intruder and delivered two 4-second bursts from short range. 'I was never any good at long-distance firing so I would always get in very close,' he explained. David saw his rounds striking the enemy aircraft, then had to bank steeply to avoid colliding with his victim. Next, Jay attacked the Heinkel and fired a long burst from 200 yards and another from 50 yards.

The attacks left the German aircraft in serious trouble. 'I could see petrol streaming from both wings, like a plume. The port engine had stopped and the undercarriage dropped down – that always seemed to happen when a Heinkel's hydraulic system was damaged. The aircraft went into a steep diving turn into cloud and disappeared from our view,' David remembered.

Although the RAF pilots did not see it crash, they were certain the Heinkel would not get home. It didn't. Before it crashed the badly shot-up bomber put out an SOS. A rescue floatplane was scrambled from Cherbourg to search for it, but no trace was found of the plane or its five-man crew. That Heinkel was the first aircraft to fall on 15 September, the first of 85 lost by both sides in one of the most intensive air actions ever fought.

Portrait of Pilot Officer Dennis David drawn by war artist William Rothenstein.

ROYAL AIR FORCE FIGHTER COMMAND UNITS, 6 pm, 14 September 1940

(First figure aircraft serviceable, second figure aircraft unserviceable)

No 10 Group, HQ Box, Wiltshire
Middle Wallop Sector

Squadron	Aircraft	Svc	Unsvc	Base
238 Squadron	Hurricanes	17	1	Middle Wallop
609 Squadron	Spitfires	15	3	Middle Wallop
604 Squadron	Blenheims	5	14	Middle Wallop
	Beaufighters	–	1	Middle Wallop
Half of 23 Squadron	Blenheims	6	–	Middle Wallop
152 Squadron	Spitfires	17	2	Warmwell
56 Squadron	Hurricanes	17	–	Boscombe Down

Filton Sector
79 Squadron	Hurricanes	13	5	Pembrey

Exeter Sector
87 Squadron	Hurricanes	17	4	Exeter
601 Squadron	Hurricanes	14	6	Exeter

St Eval Sector
234 Squadron	Spitfires	16	1	St Eval
247 Squadron	Gladiators	9	–	Roborough
(one flight only)				

No 11 Group, HQ Uxbridge, Middlesex
Kenley Sector

Squadron	Aircraft	Svc	Unsvc	Base
253 Squadron	Hurricanes	14	3	Kenley
501 Squadron	Hurricanes	18	1	Kenley
605 Squadron	Hurricanes	16	3	Croydon

Biggin Hill Sector
72 Squadron	Spitfires	10	7	Biggin Hill
92 Squadron	Spitfires	16	1	Biggin Hill
141 Squadron	Defiants	10	–	Biggin Hill
66 Squadron	Spitfires	14	2	Gravesend

Northolt Sector
1 RCAF Sqn	Hurricanes	15	3	Northolt
229 Squadron	Hurricanes	19	–	Northolt
303 Polish Sqn	Hurricanes	15	4	Northolt
264 Squadron	Defiants	8	–	Northolt
504 Squadron	Hurricanes	15	–	Hendon

Hornchurch Sector
603 Squadron	Spitfires	14	5	Hornchurch
600 Squadron	Blenheims	13	5	Hornchurch
	Beaufighters	6	6	Hornchurch
41 Squadron	Spitfires	12	6	Rochford
222 Squadron	Spitfires	11	3	Rochford

North Weald Sector
249 Squadron	Hurricanes	17	1	North Weald
Half of 23 Squadron	Blenheims	7	5	North Weald
	Beaufighters	5	–	North Weald
46 Squadron	Hurricanes	14	3	Stapleford Tawney

Debden Sector
17 Squadron	Hurricanes	15	3	Debden
73 Squadron	Hurricanes	14	–	Castle Camps
257 Squadron	Hurricanes	14	4	Martlesham Heath
Half of 25 Squadron	Blenheims	5	5	Martlesham Heath

Tangmere Sector
213 Squadron	Hurricanes	13	6	Tangmere
607 Squadron	Hurricanes	19	1	Tangmere
602 Squadron	Spitfires	15	4	Westhampnett
Half of 23 Squadron	Blenheims	10	5	Ford
	Beaufighters	1	–	Ford

No 12 Group, HQ Watnall, Nottinghamshire
Duxford Sector

Squadron	Aircraft	Svc	Unsvc	Base
242 Squadron	Hurricanes	17	–	Duxford
310 Czech Sqn	Hurricanes	18	2	Duxford
312 Czech Sqn	Hurricanes	4	5	Duxford (Non-operational)
19 Squadron	Spitfires	14	–	Fowlmere

Coltishall Sector
74 Squadron	Spitfires	14	8	Coltishall

Wittering Sector
1 Squadron	Hurricanes	16	2	Wittering
266 Squadron	Spitfires	14	5	Wittering

Digby Sector
611 Squadron	Spitfires	17	1	Digby. Moved to Fowlmere, morning 15th
151 Squadron	Hurricanes	17	1	Digby
29 Squadron	Blenheims	16	5	Digby
	Beaufighters	1	–	Digby

Kirton-in-Lindsey Sector
616 Squadron	Spitfires	14	4	Kirton-in-Lindsey
264 Squadron	Defiants	6	4	Kirton-in-Lindsey
307 Polish Sqn	Defiants	8	8	Kirton-in-Lindsey (Forming)

Church Fenton Sector
85 Squadron	Hurricanes	17	1	Church Fenton
306 Polish Sqn	Hurricanes	4	5	Church Fenton (One Flight operational)
302 Polish Sqn	Hurricanes	16	2	Leconfield. Moved to Duxford early on 15th
64 Squadron	Spitfires	7	3	Leconfield
		6	3	Ringway

No 13 Group, HQ Newcastle, Northumberland
Catterick Sector

Squadron	Aircraft	Svc	Unsvc	Base
54 Squadron	Spitfires	15	2	Catterick
Half of 219 Squadron	Blenheims	8	4	Catterick
	Beaufighters	–	1	Catterick

Usworth Sector
43 Squadron	Hurricanes	13	1	Usworth
32 Squadron	Hurricanes	14	1	Acklington
610 Squadron	Spitfires	4	5	Acklington
Half of 219 Squadron	Blenheims	6	1	Acklington

Turnhouse Sector
3 Squadron	Hurricanes	15	3	Turnhouse
65 Squadron	Spitfires	15	5	Turnhouse
141 Squadron	Defiants	7	4	Turnhouse
615 Squadron	Hurricanes	16	6	Prestwick
111 Squadron	Hurricanes	24	2	Drem
263 Squadron	Hurricanes	8	4	Drem
	Whirlwinds	4	3	Non-operational

Dyce Sector
145 Squadron	Hurricanes	13	8	Dyce

Wick Sector
232 Squadron	Hurricanes	7	1	Sumburgh

Aldergrove Sector
245 Squadron	Hurricanes	18	4	Aldergrove

coast of England three-quarters of an hour earlier, six had been shot down and four were limping back through cloud. Most of the fifteen Dorniers that remained in the formation had suffered battle damage.

Bomber Geschwader 76 had taken a fearful mauling. Yet, considering the loss of the escorts over the target and the overwhelming concentration of RAF fighters that engaged the formation, it is surprising that any Dornier survived. In fact, three-quarters of the bombers got home, eloquent testimony of the leadership of Major Alois Lindmayr and the discipline and flying skill of his crews. By any yardstick the raiding force had conducted a remarkably successful fighting withdrawal.

Luftwaffe combat report by Unteroffizier Ruehl of FG 53, claiming the destruction of a Spitfire south of London on the afternoon of 15 September.▼

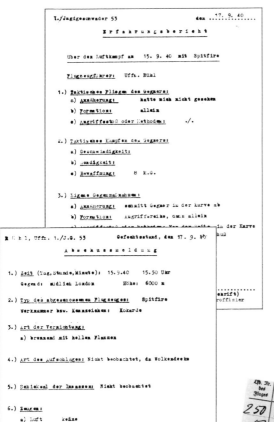

Return from London on 15 September

Feldwebel Horst Schultz, Dornier 17 pilot, Bomber Geschwader 3

'I returned to Antwerp on one engine. I did not land at my base, but at an emergency landing ground a little way away. I made a wheels-down landing on a meadow with both main wheels locked and the tyres cut to ribbons.

'As the Dornier touched down it stood on its nose, and slid along the ground on the nose and the two main wheels. When the plane came to a halt, the tail dropped to the ground with a crash. We were home!

'The radio-operator lowered the entry hatch and a stream of spent cartridge cases clattered on the grass. Carefully we lowered the wounded flight engineer to the ground and carried him about 20 metres clear of the plane. Then we lit up cigarettes – that was one of the most enjoyable I ever smoked!

'At first there was nobody around, then some civilians appeared and finally some German soldiers arrived and summoned an ambulance. With the radio-operator I walked round the aircraft to inspect the damage, stroking the trusty Dornier that had brought us home. There were more than two hundred bullet holes. I peeped inside the cowling of the starboard engine to see what was wrong with it. An entire cylinder head had been shot away and was lying in the bottom of the cowling.'

▼ **Page from the Logbook of Feldwebel Horst Schultz, a** Do 17 pilot of BG 3, who took part in the attack on London on 15 September.

RAF FIGHTER COMMAND STRENGTH SUMMARY

Group	10	11	12	13	Total
Spitfires	48	92	85	44	269
Hurricanes	78	218	109	128	533
Defiants	–	18	14	7	39
Blenheims	11	35	16	14	76
Beaufighters	–	12	1	–	13
Gladiators	9	–	–	–	9
Whirlwinds	–	–	–	4	4
TOTAL	146	375	225	197	943

As the noon raiders left the coast of England the bombers assigned to the next attack were airborne, assembled in formation and climbing towards the Pas de Calais. This raiding force was far larger than the previous one, with 114 Dorniers and Heinkels briefed to attack the Royal Victoria and West India Docks to the north of the Thames, and the Surrey Commercial Docks to the south.

Shortly before 2 pm the RAF fighter squadrons began to scramble. As an initial move, eight squadrons were ordered to patrol in pairs over Sheerness, Chelmsford, Hornchurch and Kenley.

As the vanguard of the German bomber force crossed the coast at Dungeness, the force wheeled on to a north-north-westerly heading. The move put the raiders into their planned attack formation with the three forces of bombers in line abreast about three miles apart: on the left the Dornier 17s of Bomber Geschwader 2, in the middle the Heinkel 111s of Bomber Geschwader 53 and on the right the Do 17s of Bomber Geschwader 3, followed by the He 111s of Bomber Geschwader 26. Feldwebel Heinz Kirsch of BG 3 described the mood in his Dornier as it crossed the coast: 'In our aircraft there was complete calm. The radio was silent. The safety catches were off, our steel helmets were on and each man searched his individual sector. Of the enemy there was nothing to be seen. In recent actions we had not had much contact with British fighters. We felt safe protected by the Me 109s.'

Above Romney Marsh the forward-deployed Spitfire squadrons went into action. The initial clash involved Nos 41, 92 and 222 Squadrons, with twenty-seven fighters, and these immediately became entangled with the escorting Messerschmitts.

As reports of the initial clash reached Park's headquarters his last two day fighter units, Nos 303 (Polish) and 602 Squadrons, were scrambled. All twenty-one of No 11 Group's Spitfire and Hurricane squadrons were now airborne and either in contact with the enemy or moving into position to engage. From No 12 Group, Squadron Leader Douglas Bader was again on his way south leading the five-squadron 'Big Wing'. And from the west No 10 Group sent three squadrons to protect the capital.

Fates of Germans Shot-Down on 15 September

Major Max Gruber, Heinkel 111 navigator, Bomber Geschwader 53

'After we belly-landed the Heinkel it began to burn. I tossed my papers and my pistol into the flames so they would not fall into enemy hands, then I scrambled out of the aircraft. Some soldiers arrived and started to shoot at us. We got down behind the burning aircraft and took cover. I took out my white handkerchief and waved it and the firing stopped. They approached us and I saw they were old men, Home Guard. After we were taken prisoner we were well treated. It was a Sunday afternoon, the troops took us to their headquarters and gave us tea and cakes.'

Walter Chesney, lorry driver, Streatham

'When the siren sounded, our bus came to a halt and I took cover in a doorway opposite the Oval underground station. Above us there were a lot of aircraft and a dogfight started, one of the bombers disintegrated in the air and three crewmen baled out. One of the crew came down beside the underground station. His parachute caught over electric power cables and he ended up dangling just above the ground. People came from all directions shouting "Kill him, kill him!" They pulled him down, they went crazy. Some women arrived carrying knives and pokers and they went straight in and attacked him. I felt sorry for the young lad but there was nothing one could do. In the end an army truck arrived and the half-dozen soldiers had to fight their way through the crowd to get to him. They put him in the back of the truck and drove off.'

(Fatally wounded by the mob, the German airman died soon afterwards)

◄
Major Alois Lindmayr, the commander of III/BG 76, led the formation of Dornier Do 17s that raided London at noon on 15 September. Although shortage of fuel forced the escorting Messerschmitts to turn back for home short of the target, Lindmayr continued with the bombing run and his unit delivered an accurate attack. Then he conducted a brilliant fighting withdrawal in which three-quarters of his force survived the ferocious and prolonged onslaught by a dozen squadrons of Spitfires and Hurricanes. (Rehm)

Sergeant Ray Holmes of No 504 Squadron rammed one of the Dorniers, and the bomber crashed beside Victoria Station. Holmes baled out of his fighter and landed with minor injuries. (Severnside Aviation Society, via Tutt) ▶

Its tail and outer wing panels broken off, the Dornier that Holmes had rammed spun out of the sky. Seconds after this picture was taken the aircraft crashed beside Victoria Station. (IWM) ▼

Providing Close Escort for the Bombers

Oberleutnant Hans Schmoller-Haldy, Me 109 pilot, Bomber Geschwader 54

'Sometimes we were ordered to provide close escort for a bomber formation, which I loathed. It gave the bomber crews the feeling they were being protected, and it might have deterred some of the enemy pilots. But for us fighter pilots it was very bad. We needed the advantages of altitude and speed so we could engage the enemy on favourable terms. As it was, the British fighters had the initiative of when and how to attack.

'The Heinkels cruised at about 4,000 metres [13,000ft] at about 300km/h [190mph]. On close escort we flew at about 370km/h [230mph], weaving from side to side to keep station on them. We needed to maintain speed, otherwise the Me 109s would have taken too long to accelerate to fighting speed if we were bounced by Spitfires.

'I hated having to fly direct escort. We had to stay with the bombers until our formation came under attack. When we saw the British fighters approaching we would want to accelerate to engage them. But our commander would call, "Everybody stay with the bombers." We handed to the enemy the initiative of when and how they would attack us. Until they did we had to stay close to the bombers, otherwise their people would complain and there would be recriminations when we got back.'

To defend London Fighter Command had amassed a total of 276 Spitfires and Hurricanes, slightly more than during the noontime engagement. But the German raiding force was more than twice as large as the earlier one, and outnumbered the British fighters by more than two to one. In terms of fighters, there were three Me 109s for every two Spitfires and Hurricanes.

The second wave of fighters to go into action comprised Nos 607 and 213 Squadrons, with twenty-three Hurricanes. Avoiding the escorts, they charged head-on into the Dorniers of BG 3. Pilot Officer Paddy Stephenson of No 607 Squadron loosed off a short burst at one of the Do 17s and was about to pull up to pass close over the top of his target, when he found another Hurricane blocking his escape route. Rather than collide with a friend, he held his course and rammed one of the Dorniers. The Hurricane reared up out of control, rolled on its back and went down in a steep inverted dive. Stephenson jumped clear of the stricken fighter. Meanwhile the shattered Dornier was also spinning out of control and plunged into a small wood near Kilndown with its crew.

The battle around the bombers continued, as the Hurricanes split into sections and curved round to join the Spitfires attempting to engage the bombers from astern and from the flanks. Again and again the Messerschmitts came diving in to break up the attacks or drive away the Spitfires or Hurricanes. For their part the bomber crews held tight formation and put up a powerful cross-fire whenever a British fighter came within range.

For the Messerschmitt pilots assigned to the close escort this was a particularly frustrating time. They were not permitted to pursue enemy fighters and go for a kill if it meant leaving their charges. Again and again the Me 109s had to break off the chase and return to their bombers; then the British fighters would return and the process had to be repeated.

Next to join the mêlée were Nos 605 and 501 Squadrons, with fourteen Hurricanes. And now, four minutes after the loss of its first Dornier in collision, BG 3 lost another to the same cause. As Pilot Officer Tom Cooper-Slipper closed on one of the Do 17s, an accurate burst of return fire jammed his ailerons. The Hurricane smashed into the bomber and both aircraft tumbled out of the sky. Cooper-Slipper baled out, as did the crew of the Dornier.

Feldwebel Horst Schultz, piloting one of the Dorniers, watched it all happen: 'The British fighter came in from right to left, from the rear, and rammed into the Dornier. Then I saw three parachutes appear from the two aircraft as they went down. But again I could not spend much time watching, I had to hold formation or I would be joining them . . . ' Those in the bomber formation who had observed the two collisions had no way of knowing that neither had been premeditated. Some of the watchers believed that the RAF was in such desperate straits that its pilots had orders to ram the bombers. If that was so, the tactic was proving devastatingly effective . . .

Following the initial attacks, the German escorts re-grouped and once again the action devolved into a series of short, fleeting combats between the opposing fighters. The respite for the German bomber crews would be brief, however, for now they came within range of the anti-aircraft batteries deployed along the Thames. From the south and west of Chatham a concentration of twenty 4.5in and eight 3.7in guns opened up a heavy barrage that caused damage to two bombers and forced them to leave the protection of their formations.

Now Fighter Command was at full stretch, with several squadrons in contact with the raiders and others converging on them from all directions. Winston Churchill was visiting Park's underground operations room that day, and he watched the action unfold:

'I became conscious of the anxiety of the Commander, who now stood still behind his subordinate's chair. Hitherto I had watched in silence. Now I asked: "What other reserves have we?" "There are none," said Air Vice-Marshal Park. In an account which he wrote about it afterwards he said that at this I "looked grave." Well I might. What losses should we not suffer if our refuelling planes were caught on the ground by further raids of "40 plus" or "50 plus"! The odds were great; our margins small; the stakes infinite.'

At the time of the conversation, at about 2.35 pm on that fateful Sunday afternoon, every Spitfire and Hurricane squadron in No 11

▲ Unsuccessful secret weapon: air test of the experimental flame-thrower installation fitted to the Dornier 17 flown by Feldwebel Rolf Heitsch of BG 76. The use of the weapon attracted rather than discouraged attacking fighters, however, and when it was first used in action on 15 September the Dornier was shot down and crash-landed near Sevenoaks. One of the crew was fatally wounded; Heitsch and the other two crewmen were taken prisoner. (Heitsch, via Saunders)▼

'The most serious and unpardonable error . . .'

Oberleutnant Hans Schmoller-Haldy, Me 109 pilot,
Bomber Geschwader 54

'On 23 September our mission was a free hunting sweep in the triangle Ramsgate - Canterbury - Folkestone where British fighter activity had been reported. With three of my pilots I took off at 10.27 and headed towards Ramsgate in a slow climb to 4,500 metres [about 15,000ft]. The weather was strange, with layers of cloud in which aircraft could easily hide. There were several aircraft about which we saw for a moment before they disappeared, we never knew if they were British or German. It was uncanny.

'We flew in wide curves, always changing altitude, never flying straight for long. We had been flying for 60 minutes, I thought that was enough and as we were turning for home I suddenly observed a Hurricane squadron between Ramsgate and Dover, twelve aircraft in four "pulks" one behind the other. They were about 1,000 metres below us and climbing in wide curves, like a creeping worm. My impression was that it was a Hurricane squadron on a training mission. The Hurricane pilots had no idea that four 109s were above them, like eagles looking down on their prey.

'The spectacle was so fascinating that we completely forgot what was going on around us. That is the most serious and unpardonable error a fighter pilot can commit, and catastrophe immediately followed. Four Spitfires, of which we had been unaware due to our carelessness, attacked us from out of the sun. They fired at us from behind, roared close over our heads at high speed and disappeared back into the sky. As we broke formation I saw a 109 going down in flames on my right. It was Oberfeldwebel Knipscher, we never heard what happened to him.'

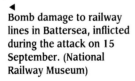

▶ Unteroffizier Figge brought his badly shot-up Dornier back to France following the noon action, and crash-landed near Poix. The bomber had more than two hundred hits from 0.303in rounds and was damaged beyond repair. The crewman wearing the field dressing and swigging at the bottle is Oberleutnant Florian, the navigator.

◀ Bomb damage to railway lines in Battersea, inflicted during the attack on 15 September. (National Railway Museum)

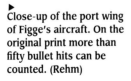

▶ Close-up of the port wing of Figge's aircraft. On the original print more than fifty bullet hits can be counted. (Rehm)

Group and the sectors immediately adjacent to it was airborne.

As during the earlier action, Park concentrated the bulk of his force immediately in front of London for the main engagement. No fewer than nineteen fresh squadrons were being moved into position to the south and east of the capital, with 185 Spitfires and Hurricanes.

Once again it was the Dornier 17s of BG 3 that bore the brunt of the attack. Heinz Kirsch remembers:

'A new call, "Fighters dead astern!" Something struck our machine. "Hit on the left elevator!" called the radio-operator. Like a couple of shadows two Hurricanes swept over us, they came past so quickly we were unable to "greet" them. More hits on our machine. And on top of that there was smoke in the cabin. The Tommies were staking everything they had, never before had we come under such heavy attack. After firing, the fighters pulled to the left or right to go past us. Some came so close I thought they were going to ram us.'

During this attack three more Do 17s were knocked out of formation. From his Me 109 Oberleutnant Hans Schmoller-Haldy, flying close escort with the Heinkel formation behind the Dorniers, watched them go down: 'There were parachutes all over the place. Several British fighters were buzzing around the Dorniers. I thought "Oh, those poor men . . ." But we couldn't do anything to help, we had to stay with our Heinkels.' Moments later Schmoller-Haldy and his comrades had their work cut out, as a squadron of Hurricanes attemped to punch through to the Heinkels.

Over London Douglas Bader's 'Big Wing' again joined the battle, but on this occasion it had been scrambled too late. The five squadrons arrived over the capital still in the climb and almost immediately came under attack from free-hunting Me 109s diving from above. Bader ordered the three Hurricane squadrons to split up and engage the enemy fighters while, in a reversal of their usual role, the Spitfires were to try to get through to the bombers. Bader's own combat report described the chaos that now ensued:

'On being attacked from behind by Me 109 I ordered break-up and pulled up and round violently. Coming off my back partially blacked out, nearly collided with Yellow 2 [Pilot Officer

THE LAST ATTACK OF PETER PEASE

OVER MAIDSTONE, 2.55 PM, 15 SEPTEMBER. Having dropped their bombs on targets in the West Ham area of London, the formation of Heinkel 111s of Bomber Geschwader 26 was heading for home. Other German units had been hit hard that day but so far BG 26 had had a clear run. Its sole loss had been a straggler forced out of formation by engine trouble and finished off by British fighters. Few Spitfires and Hurricanes came near its formation, and most of those were driven off by the escorting Messerschmitts. But, as Leutnant Roderich Cescotti recalled, there was one extremely determined exception:

'A few Tommies succeeded in penetrating our fighter escort. I saw a Spitfire dive steeply through our escort, level out and close rapidly on our formation. It opened fire, from ahead and to the right, and its tracers streaked towards us. At that moment an Me 109, which we had not seen before, appeared behind the Spitfire and we saw its rounds striking the Spitfire's tail. But the Tommy continued his attack, coming straight for us, and his rounds slashed into our aircraft. We could not return the fire for fear of hitting the Messerschmitt. I put my left arm across my face to protect it from the plexiglass splinters flying around the cockpit, holding the controls with my right hand. With only the thin plexiglass between us, we were eye to eye with the enemy's eight machine guns. At the last moment the Spitfire pulled up and passed very close over the top of us. Then it rolled on its back, as though out of control, and went down steeply, trailing black smoke. Waggling its wings, the Messerschmitt swept past us and curved in for another attack. The action lasted only a few seconds, but it demonstrated the determination and bravery with which the Tommies were fighting over their own country.'

Although his bomber had taken several hits, Cescotti held position in formation and got home safely.

The courageous Spitfire pilot was Flying Officer Peter Pease of No 603 Squadron who was shot down at a time and place, and in a manner, consistent with Cescotti's account. Pease was still in the cockpit of his blazing fighter when it dived into the ground a few miles south-east of Maidstone.

The son of Sir Richard Pease, of Richmond, Yorkshire, Arthur Peter Pease studied at Eton and Cambridge University before joining the RAF at the beginning of the war. In July 1940 he was posted to No 603 Squadron then based at Aberdeen Dyce. He and another of the new pilots sent to the squadron at that time, Richard Hillary, had struck up a firm friendship. In his book *The Last Enemy*, one of the classic works on the Battle of Britain, Hillary would later write:

'Peter was, I think, the best looking man I have ever seen. He stood six foot three and was of a deceptive slightness, for he weighed close on thirteen stone. He had an outward reserve which protected him from any surface friendships, but for those who troubled to get to know him it was apparent that this reserve masked a deep shyness and a profound integrity of character. Soft spoken, and with an innate habit of understatement, I never knew him to lose his temper. He never spoke of himself, and it was only through Colin that I learned how well he had done at Eton before his two reflective years at Cambridge, where he had watched events in Europe and made up his mind what part he must play when the exponents of everything he abhorred began to sweep all before them.'

On 30 July Peter Pease was credited with a half share in the destruction of a Heinkel 111. Early the following month No 603 Squadron moved to Hornchurch and was thrown into action. Hillary wrote: 'Twenty-four of us flew south that tenth day of August 1940; of those twenty-four, eight were to fly back.'

Neither Richard Hillary nor Peter Pease would be numbered among those survivors. Hillary was shot down in flames on 3 September, and rescued from the sea with terrible burns. Pease was credited with shooting down an Me 109 during the same action. On the 7th he had a narrow escape when his Spitfire was damaged in action over London, and he was forced to make a crash-landing at Hornchurch. Just over a week later, on 15 September, Pease went down in his blazing Spitfire.

Pilot Officer Peter Pease of No 603 Squadron, pilot of the Spitfire, who was shot down and killed immediately after the attack. (Sir Richard Pease)

Leutnant Roderich Cescotti, of BG 26, never forgot the brave attack by the lone Spitfire on his formation on 15 September. (Cescotti)

The front page of the *Daily Express* on 16 September 1940, describing the hard-fought actions on the previous day and repeating the Air Ministry claim that 175 German planes had been shot down. During the 16th the Air Ministry issued a revised bulletin which stated that, after a recount, the number of enemy aircraft destroyed was 185. Following examination of German records after the war, we know that both figures were massive overclaims: in fact the Luftwaffe had lost only fifty-eight aircraft. But although the German losses fell far short of those claimed, the action fought on 15 September decided the outcome of the Battle. Recognizing that victory was not in his grasp before the weather broke in the autumn, on 17 September Hitler ordered that Operation 'Sealion' – the planned invasion of southern England – be postponed until further notice. The threat would never return.

Daily Express

SETS THE SEAL ON ANY MEAL — H-P SAUCE

BLACK OUT ZERO HOUR TO-NIGHT UNTIL 6.9 A.M. MOON RISES / MOON SETS

One Penny

Monday, September 16, 1940

No. 12,579

Sunday raids on London by 400 planes

R.A.F. smash Goering's

175 SHOT DOWN

Another bomb on Palace

5 RAIDERS CRASH ON LONDON

Fifth hospital bombed

SECOND WEEK OF THE BATTLE OF LONDON WAS OPENED BY GOERING WITH FOUR MORE BIG DAY AND NIGHT RAIDS—AND BY THE R.A.F. WITH A SMASHING VICTORY.

This morning it was learned that 175 enemy aircraft, out of 400 sent in many waves, were shot down in the three Sunday daylight raids on London. Thirty R.A.F. fighters were lost, but the pilots of ten are safe.

Again the Nazi murder bombs were sent against Buckingham Palace in a third deliberate attempt to kill the King and Queen. One bomb, which did not explode, damaged the Queen's private apartment.

Vengeance was swift. Almost immediately afterwards the plane which bombed the Palace was shot to pieces in mid-air by Spitfires.

Great air battles were fought out fiercely all the way from the coast to London as big formations of British fighters sailed into the massed squadrons which tried to fight their way to the capital.

And all the way from the coast to London the countryside is strewn with the wreckage of shot down Nazi bombers.

AT LEAST FIVE CAME DOWN IN LONDON. ONE EXPLODED IN THE AIR AND CRASHED ON TO A JEWELLER'S SHOP BESIDE VICTORIA STATION.

On each raid a few of the bombers reached London and dropped bombs at random, particularly in the east and south-east. Although losses were hit there were few casualties.

German air force losses for the first time in days of the Blitz. It began on Saturday last week—now reach this staggering total:—

PLANES LOST 455
AIRMEN LOST 1,100

Only fifty-seven pilots, the others landing safely after baling out.

The German version of their losses yesterday is, as usual, incredibly underestimated. They say they shot sixty British planes down and a two of our airplanes failed to return.

In the raid last night and early this morning bombs were dropped on one of London's most famous hospitals—the fifth hospital to be hit—a London theatre, a newspaper office, and a large block of offices. A large number of houses also were hit.

All the time the R.A.F. continue their terrific attack on Hitler's invasion bases. Again on Saturday night they dropped hundreds of tons of explosives on the Channel ports.

Spitfires ambush raiders

SPITFIRES and Hurricanes, lying hidden in clouds, and working in perfect conjunction with ground batteries, darted from their sky ambush yesterday to smash attacks by 400 German raiders in two big battles.

New tricks and tactics had the Germans bewildered and baffled.

The R.A.F. fighters handed them on from ambush to ambush. Anti-aircraft gunners helped to head the raiders into clouds where more Spitfires were waiting.

Besides doing this, the ground gunners knocked off at least four raiders' to add to their own score.

The wrecking of the Germans began the moment they crossed the Kent coast before noon.

For several weeks the outer ring of British fighters that patrolled several miles inland, and the raiders have got used to meeting only ground fire on flying across the Channel coasts.

But as Dornier bombers, with Messerschmitt 109's circling above to screen them, swooped through clouds beneath the Straits of Dover, Hurricanes pounced on them from all directions.

One Dornier went down. Two Messerschmitts followed. The rest scattered.

In a little less than half an hour the Messerschmitts fought are rearward action. Then they fled out to sea in twos and threes, following the beaten bombers.

In all, eight or ten groups of Nazis came over in this attack, between Dover and Dungeness. Only two formations got through towards London, and they crossed the first attack at 11.34 a.m. It lasted till 12.30.

Fine co-operation between gunners below and fighters above was seen when formation of Spitfires approached London.

About thirty Spitfires suddenly shot out of a tank of cloud. Two Nazi planes crashed. The rest scattered for the cover of the clouds to the east.

A curtain of shells shot up in front of raiders, making like a flock of frightened birds—and then made off a few formation of Spitfires which had been lurking in another cloud.

Two more Germans were seen to crash. The rest scattered with the Spitfires and Hurricanes blazing away. Spitfire and Hurricane squadrons chased the remnants away from Maidstone and Canterbury above the Medway and...

I WATCH THE R.A.F. BLITZ

Daily Express Staff Reporter SEFTON DELMER   DOVER, Sunday.

A LIGHT mist hangs over the Channel. The sea is fairly calm and the clouds overhead are thick, billowy and high up. They have those little blue patches in between them which Goering's bombers like particularly. In other words, it is good invasion weather over the Channel.

But, and you may think I am a pessimist for saying so, I can't see them coming yet. There is still so much to discourage them.

There is all that R.A.F. us in the sky shooting down the German raiders over the flat land and into the sea, as I have seen them shooting them up to-day. The raiding isn't exactly what you'd call empty.

And then there is what I saw going on last night and what I have finished telephoning this morning. I shall be watching again to-night: all-night bombing of the German bases on the French coast. But you could not think up a more tonic experience for me one so have, from one of the bombed districts of London.

It was before nine, probably about the time the sirens went in London and you went down into your shelters. They certainly were the sirens were going on in London and they certainly were over in Calais and Boulogne and Dunkirk.

MYSTERY TRACERS

I saw the bombs flashing bright and white as they exploded. I saw the parachute flares like orange stars shooting in the air, then lighting up the objective during the storm. The barges, the quay the docks, the troops, the searchlights stabbed up into the darkness, then from Calais came being snaked out of the anti-aircraft guns fired and from bullets...

WHERE RAIDERS DIE

Now was last night's particularly big show. They have been getting the same...

PALACE LAWNS SET ON FIRE

Daily Express Staff Reporter HILDE MARCHANT

ONCE again the German Air Force has attacked Buckingham Palace. This is the third attempt to kill the King and Queen or drive them from London to back up his own communiqués.

Two high explosive bombs were dropped. One landed in a bath, and falling masonry damaged the Queen's drawing-room.

The second, a small time bomb, landed in the grounds. It went off later in the day.

Fifteen incendiary bombs were also dropped, alighting on lawns and bushes. Small fires broke out, but police and Palace A.R.P. staff put them out rapidly.

The attack this time did not go unpunished. One of the raiders was blown to pieces in the air by a Spitfire.

Passers-by high heard the sight planes flying thrilled to the sight of the British fighter sailing in to battle the bombs...

BOMB CRASHES DOWN HOSPITAL STAIRS

Daily Express Raid Reporters

ONE of the oldest London hospitals was hit by a bomb last night. The bomb fell down the main staircase and shattered it—but not one of the patients in the wards leading off the stairs was injured.

Only one person was injured—a member of the medical staff who was in a small room at the top of the building.

A volunteer fireman climbed a ladder and brought him down from the top...

London theatre bombed

And large block of offices

A London theatre was badly damaged early today when a bomb fell on a large block of offices.

It is believed that a number of phone operators and a number of workers were in the offices.

£5,046,966 given for aircraft

The Minister of Aircraft Production announced last night that gifts from the public in Britain and overseas for the purchase of £5,046,966, have reached the total of £5,046,966.

He urged everyone to buy a Spitfire.

CHANNEL WEATHER:—Strong N.W. breeze at Dover yesterday: off shore breeze at dusk. Bright moon, high cloud.

A NAZI bomber taking part in the Sunday raids on London is shot down in flames in the middle of Streatham High Road. In the shop the flats on either side of the street. Large pieces of flying stone shattered windows as far as 200 yards away.

Crowley-Milling]. Spun off his slipstream and straightened out 5,000 feet below without firing a shot. Climbed up again and saw E/A twin-engined flying westwards. Just got in range and fired a short burst (3 secs) in a completely stalled position and then spun off again and lost more height.'

The 'Big Wing' was unable to deliver the hoped-for concerted attack on a bomber formation but, by its presence, it tied down several of the enemy free-hunting patrols and made it easier for other British squadrons to reach the bombers.

While the German covering force was thus engaged, four squadrons (Nos 1 Canadian, 66, 72 and 229) ran in to attack the Heinkels of BG 53. Squadron Leader Rupert Leigh led nine Spitfires of No 66 Squadron against the bombers while two 'weavers' provided top cover to hold off any Messerschmitts that might attempt to interfere. Flight Lieutenant Bob Oxspring, in one of the covering Spitfires, recalled: 'While the others went in to attack, I was a bit concerned about some Me 109s above me and did a 360-degree turn to ward them off. I climbed to get more altitude in case there was a fight, being careful not to lose speed in the process . . . never get caught by the enemy at climbing speed, that is the worst thing that can happen.'

While Oxspring kept a wary eye on the enemy fighters, Leigh ordered the other Spitfires into line astern, went into a shallow dive to build up speed, then pulled up steeply to attack the Heinkels from in front and below – the quarter where their defensive armament was weakest. Spitfire after Spitfire ran in to short range, fired a brief burst then broke away. High above, Bob Oxspring watched the Messerschmitts continue on unconcernedly. 'They did not seem about to interfere so I went down after the rest of the squadron and attacked one of the bombers from out of the sun. With 0.303in ammunition you never knew if you had hit an enemy aircraft, unless you saw a flash or some obvious form of damage. The Heinkel broke away from the formation. I continued on, going down fast, and went through the formation.'

Next the Spitfires of No 72 Squadron attacked, followed by the Hurricanes of Nos 1 (Canadian) and 229 Squadrons. One of the bombers caught a lethal burst, it is not clear from whom, and fell out of the sky trailing smoke and flame. It smashed into open ground at Woolwich Arsenal; there were no survivors. Two other Heinkels, less seriously damaged, were forced to turn for home.

The escorting Messerschmitts, drawn from FG 3, fought back resolutely to defend their charges and Leutnant Detlev Rohwer claimed the destruction of one of the attacking Hurricanes during this action. Probably his victim

---

'The whole world seemed to be tumbling in'

Pilot Officer Erick Marrs, Spitfire pilot, No 152 Squadron describing his action on 30 September

'We were just going in to attack when somebody yelled "Messer-schmitts" over the R/T and the whole squadron split up. Actually it was a false alarm. Anyway, being on my own I debated what to do. The bombers were my object, so I snooped in under the 110s and attacked the bombers (about 40-50 Heinkel 111s) from the starboard beam.

'I got in a burst of about three seconds when – Crash! and the whole world seemed to be tumbling in on me. I pushed the stick forward hard, went into a vertical dive and held it until I was below cloud. I had a look round. The chief trouble was that petrol was gushing into the cockpit at the rate of gallons all over my feet, and there was a sort of lake of petrol in the bottom of the cockpit. My knee and leg were tingling all over as if I had pushed them into a bed of nettles. There was a bullet hole in my windscreen where a bullet had come in and entered the dashboard, knocking away the starter button. Another bullet, I think an explosive one, had knocked away one of my petrol taps in front of the joystick, spattering my leg with little splinters and sending a chunk of something through the backside of my petrol tank near the bottom. I had obviously run into some pretty good crossfire from the Heinkels. I made for home at top speed to get there before all my petrol ran out. I was about 15 miles from the aerodrome and it was a heart-rending business with all that petrol gushing over my legs and the constant danger of fire. About five miles from the 'drome smoke began to come from under my dashboard. I thought the whole thing might blow up at any minute, so I switched off my engine. The smoke stopped, I glided towards the 'drome and tried putting my wheels down. One came down and the other remained stuck up. I tried to get the one that was down up again. It was stuck down. There was nothing for it but to make a one-wheel landing. I switched on my engine again to make the aerodrome. It took me some way and then began to smoke again, so I hastily switched off. I was now near enough and made a normal approach and held off. I made a good landing, touching down lightly. The unsupported wing slowly began to drop. I was able to hold it up for some time and then down came the wing tip on the ground. I began to slew round and counteracted as much as possible with the brake on the wheel which was down. I ended up going sideways on one wheel, a tail wheel and a wing tip. Luckily, the good tyre held out and the only damage to the aeroplane, apart from that done by the bullets, is a wing tip which is easily replaceable.

'I hopped out and went off to the M.O. to get a lot of metal splinters picked out of my leg and wrist. I felt jolly glad to be down on the ground without having caught fire.'

ADOLF GALLAND'S 33rd VICTORY

OVER BILLERICAY, 3 PM, 15 SEPTEMBER. Leading Messerschmitt Me 109s of Fighter Geschwader 26 on a free-hunting sweep in support of bombers attacking London, Major Adolf Galland became embroiled with a squadron of Hurricanes. In his combat report on the action he later wrote:

'After an unsuccessful ten minute dogfight with about eight Hurricanes, during which much altitude was lost, with the Staff flight I attacked two Hurricanes about 800m below us. Maintaining surprise, I closed on the wing man and opened fire from 120m as he was in a gentle turn to the left. The enemy plane reeled as my rounds struck the nose from below, and pieces fell from the left wing and fuselage. The left side of the fuselage burst into flame. The enemy section leader was shot down in flames by my wing man, Oberleutnant Horten.'

Galland's victory, his 33rd, had followed a classic surprise attack from his victim's blind zone. The Hurricanes belonged to No 310 (Czech) Squadron and the subsequent report of the pilot Galland had attacked, Sergeant J. Hubacek, makes it clear he never even saw his assailant.

' . . . I climbed again and at about 18,000ft I had the impression that I heard machine gun fire behind me. I looked back several times but I did not see anything. I retrimmed the aircraft, but at that moment I was hit – I do not know by what – the cockpit was full of smoke but I did not see any fire. The aircraft turned first to the right and then went slowly into a spin.'

Hubacek baled out and landed with injuries to his right foot. Squadron Leader A. Hess, the Commander of No 310 Squadron, was pilot of the Hurricane that Horten shot down. He too baled out, and landed without injury. Both British fighters crashed near Billericay.

▲ Adolf Galland in his personal Messerschmitt 109, the aircraft in which he scored his thirty-third victory on 15 September. (via Schliephake)

▼ Major Adolf Galland, seated second from left, with pilots of FG 26, beside his headquarters caravan at Caffiers near Calais. (Schoepfel)

was Flying Officer Yuile of No 1 (Canadian) Squadron, who later wrote:

'We were diving in to attack a formation of Heinkels. I was so intent on watching the bombers that I forgot for a moment that we were supposed to have eyes in the side and back of our heads, as well as in front. A Messerschmitt that I had failed to notice flashed down on my tail and the next thing I knew something hit me in the shoulder with the force of a sledgehammer. An armour-piercing bullet had penetrated the armour plate of the cockpit and got me. I was momentarily numbed, and when I swung round the German had gone.'

Yuile broke off the action and managed to get his damaged fighter back to Northolt and land there.

On the way to the target four German bombers had been shot down, and seven damaged to such an extent that they were forced to leave formation and turn for home. All five formations of bombers reached London intact, however, and now they lined up for bombing runs on their assigned targets in the dock areas.

During the day the cloud cover over southern England had built up appreciably, and now most of the capital was concealed under nine-tenths cumulus and strato-cumulus cloud with its base at about 2,000 feet and the tops extending to 12,000 feet. All the briefed targets were enshrouded in cloud. To the north of the Thames the only clear patch of sky was over West Ham, and two formations of Heinkels and one of Dorniers realigned their runs and released their bombs on the borough. Throughout the area there was widespread damage.

Meanwhile the two formations of Dorniers of BG 2, prevented by cloud from attacking the Surrey Commercial Docks to the south of the river, turned through a semi-circle without bombing and headed east. For pilots of the three Hurricane squadrons battling with the escorts around this part of the raiding force, the U-turn was an unexpected delight. Several RAF pilots were convinced that by their presence they had scared the Germans into turning back from the capital, and afterwards they would say so in their combat reports. In fact, both Dornier formations had reached the capital intact, having lost only one aircraft on the

way in, and would easily have fought through to their briefed target had they been able to see it. On their way home the Dorniers scattered their bombs over several districts and there were reports of damage in the Penge, Bexley, Crayford, Dartford and Orpington areas.

Bombers that had become detached from their formations now picked their way through the banks of cloud over Kent, playing a deadly game of hide-and-seek with enemy fighters. Leutnant Herburt Michaelis of BG 2, flying his Do 17 home on one engine, emerged from a patch of cloud and was immediately spotted by Squadron Leader John Sample of No 504 Squadron. In his account of the action the Hurricane pilot later wrote:

'I started to chase one Dornier which was flying through the tops of clouds . . . I attacked him four times altogether. When he first appeared through the cloud – you know how clouds go up and down like foam on water – I fired at him from the left, swung over to the right, turned in towards another hollow in the cloud where I expected him to reappear, and fired at him again.'

One of Sample's attacks shattered the bomber's glass nose, and a round passed through Michaelis's life-jacket, tearing away the pouch containing the yellow dye marker (to mark his position if he came down in the sea). The fine dust flew everywhere and some went into the German pilot's eyes, blinding him temporarily. Michaelis ordered his crew to bale out, groped his way to the escape hatch and followed. The bomber crashed near Dartford.

At 3.25 pm the 'tote board' on the wall of the No 11 Group operations room at Uxbridge revealed that No 213 Squadron at Tangmere was again ready for action, its Hurricanes refuelled and rearmed. Once again Park had a fighting reserve, albeit a slender one. The RAF commander had thrown into action every Spitfire and Hurricane he could lay his hands on, and the gamble had paid off. During the minutes that followed other squadrons reported themselves 'At Readiness.' The crisis was over.

Despite the extensive cloud cover and the delay in scrambling the 'Big Wing,' in general the RAF fighter controllers performed their task in exemplary fashion that afternoon.

▲ The Supermarine works at Woolston on the outskirts of Southampton, abandoned after the attack on 26 September. (via Scrope)

▶▼ Outside and inside of Anna Valley Motors of Salisbury, typical of the workshops in Hampshire, Wiltshire and Berkshire into which Spitfire production was dispersed after the main factories were bombed. This unit produced wing leading edges. (via Scrope)

KEEPING THE SPITFIRES COMING

On 26 September a force of 59 Heinkel 111s of Bomber Geschwader 55 delivered a devastating attack on the Supermarine factories at Woolston and Itchen on the outskirts of Southampton, responsible for the majority of Spitfire production. At the factories most of the machine tools and production jigs had survived, however, and the final assembly hangars at Eastleigh were untouched.

On the day following the attack Lord Beaverbrook, the Minister of Aircraft Production, visited Southampton to inspect the damage. He ordered that the two wrecked factories be abandoned and Spitfire production to be dispersed into the surrounding area. During the following week Supermarine executives toured the Southampton, Winchester, Salisbury, Trowbridge, Reading and Newbury areas, examining large open buildings such as motor repair garages, laundries, bus stations, etc. Accompanying each executive was a policeman with a letter of introduction from the Chief Constable, requesting co-operation but giving no reason for the visit. Where premises were considered suitable for the dispersed production scheme, the not-always-delighted owner was served with official papers to requisition the building. As each site was acquired, Spitfire production jigs and machine tools were moved in from the shattered factories.

By the end of October thirty-five separate premises were taken over for the Spitfire programme and production had begun at sixteen of them. Also by this time, large-scale production of these fighters had started at the huge new Nuffield Organization factory at Castle Bromwich near Birmingham. Never again would Spitfire production be as vulnerable to air attack as it had been in September 1940.

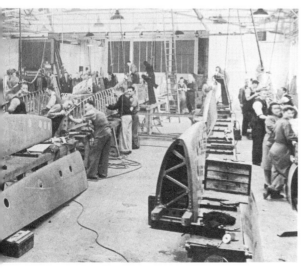

▲ By the end of September Spitfire production was getting into its stride at the new Nuffield plant at Castle Bromwich near Birmingham, and that month the factory turned out fifty-six aircraft. (IWM)

▶ Winston Churchill pictured during a visit to Castle Bromwich, chatting to Alex Henshaw, the Chief Test Pilot at the works. (Henshaw)

Round the Clock Bombing: Main Attacks on Britain, 15 Sept 1940

Time of attack	Target attacked	Unit	Attacking force	Remarks
Midnight	London	KGr 606	13 Do 17	In progress at midnight
0.15 am	London	KG 51	2 Ju 88	Night attack
0.50 am	London	KGr 126	11 He 111	As above
2.00 am	London	KG 4	5 He 111	Night attack planned for 46 bombers. Operation curtailed due to bad weather over bases in Holland
11.50 am	London	II/LG 2	21 Me 109	Attack by fighter-bombers
12.10 pm	London	I & III/BG 76	25 Do 17	Attacked rail viaducts at Battersea
2.45 pm	London	II/BG 3	20 He 111	Intended target, Royal Victoria docks, could not be attacked due to cloud. Bombed West Ham area instead
2.48 pm	London	II/BG 3	11 Do 17	As above
2.50 pm	London	I & II/BG 26	27 He 111	Intended target West India Docks. Bombed Bromley-by-Bow gas works instead
2.55 pm	London	II & III/BG 2	42 Do 17	Intended target Surrey Commercial Docks. Bombed targets of opportunity in SE London and Kent instead
3.30 pm	Portland	I & III/BG 55	26 He 111	RN dockyard
5.30 pm	Southampton	EGr 210	10 Me 110 3 Me 109	Target Supermarine aircraft factory. Bombs missed target and fell on built-up area nearby
8.00 pm	London	BGr 806	7 Ju 88	Night attack
8.50 pm	London	III/LG 1	10 Ju 88	As above
9.05 pm	London	II/BG 55	15 He 111	As above
9.46 pm	London	I/LG 1	10 Ju 88	As above
10.25 pm	London	St & I/BG 55	5 He 111	As above
10.45 pm	London	III/BG 27	11 He 111	As above
10.48 pm	Liverpool	II/BG 27	9 He 111	As above
11.12 pm	London	I/BG 54	10 Ju 88	As above
11.32 pm	London	I/BG 27	18 He 111	As above
11.50 pm	London	II/BG 51	8 Ju 88	As above

Abbreviations:
BG – Bomber Geschwader   BGr – Bomber Gruppe
LG – Lehrgeschwader   EGr – Erprobungsgruppe
St – Staff Flight
I & III/BG 55 – Ist and IIIrd Gruppen of Bomber Gruppe 55

▶ **Luftwaffe flying map of Great Britain.**

Twenty-eight squadrons of Spitfires and Hurricanes were scrambled, and every one went into action.

Elsewhere that afternoon Heinkel 111s of BG 55 attacked the Royal Navy base at Portland and a small force of Messerschmitt 109 and 110 fighter-bombers of Erprobungsgruppe 210 tried unsuccessfully to hit the Supermarine aircraft works at Woolston near Southampton.

Neither attack caused significant damage to military targets.

During the hard-fought actions on the 15th the Luftwaffe lost 58 aircraft, as against the 29 lost by RAF Fighter Command. Although the German loss fell far short of the 185 aircraft claimed destroyed by the defences at the time, the day's fighting decided the outcome of the Battle. On 17 September Hitler ordered that

Operation 'Sealion', the planned invasion of southern England, be postponed until further notice. Within days the ships and barges that had been concentrated at ports along the Channel coast started to disperse. From then on the threat of invasion diminished with each day that passed.

On the 18th there was an unsuccessful daylight attack on the capital, and others on the 27th and 28th. Also during the latter part of the month the Luftwaffe carried out destructive attacks on the Bristol Aeroplane Co works near Bristol (on the 25th) and the Supermarine works at Southampton (on the 26th). Yet the era of the massed attack by twin-engined bombers by day was drawing to a close. Following the hectic battle of the 15th, the German High Command knew that victory against the RAF no longer lay within its grasp.

During this phase of the battle the Luftwaffe lost a total of 411 aircraft, while the RAF lost 238 fighters. That gave an overall loss ratio of 1.7:1 in favour of the RAF, slightly greater than during the previous phase in spite of the relatively poor showing by the defenders at the beginning of the period. Although the capital had taken a battering there was no breakdown in civilian morale, and Fighter Command had demonstrated that the reports of its impending demise had been greatly exaggerated. The outcome of the Battle had been decided and for the Germans it was now a question of maintaining the pressure on Britain, while the Fuehrer decided on his next move.

THE ATTACK ON LONDON – AIRCRAFT LOSSES

Note: On each night during this period there was a large-scale attack on London, and on some nights other cities were attacked also.

	Luftwaffe	RAF	Main Daylight Action
7 September	40	21	Heavy attack on London docks
8 September	14	6	Attacks on airfields
9 September	25	18	Poor weather, unsuccessful attack on London
10 September	4	1	Little activity
11 September	24	28	Attack on London
12 September	4	0	Little activity
13 September	4	3	Little activity
14 September	10	12	Attack on London
15 September	56	29	Two attacks on London
16 September	8	1	Little activity
17 September	8	6	Little activity
18 September	18	13	Attack on London
19 September	9	0	Poor weather, little activity
20 September	9	8	Poor weather, little activity
21 September	9	0	Little activity
22 September	3	1	Poor weather, little activity
23 September	14	11	Fighter sweeps over SE England
24 September	12	4	Little activity
25 September	14	3	Attack on Bristol aircraft works
26 September	7	8	Attack on Supermarine aircraft works at Southampton
27 September	55	28	Attack on London
28 September	10	16	Attacks on London
29 September	8	6	Little activity
30 September	46	18	Attack on Westland aircraft works at Yeovil
TOTALS	411	241	

Spitfires of Nos 603 ('XT' code letters) and 222 ('ZD') Squadrons at Hornchurch during the Battle of Britain. Note the steam roller in the background, used to flatten the bomb craters after they had been filled with rubble. (Crown Copyright) ▼

4. NIGHT BLITZ AND TIP-AND-RUN RAIDS
1 October to 1 November

'I have night's dark cloak to hide me from their eyes.'
Shakespeare: 'Romeo and Juliet'

AT THE BEGINNING OF OCTOBER, having abandoned daylight attacks on Britain, the German bomber force confined itself almost entirely to night raids. And against these, as we have seen, the defenders had no effective counter. Unless bombers were held and illuminated by searchlights for half a minute or more, the anti-aircraft gun batteries had no means of locating the night raiders accurately enough to carry through an engagement. Even when they worked, the few available radars were little help. The Gunlaying Mark I radar had been designed to give only range information, and it did that well enough; but the bearings it gave were inaccurate and it gave no indication of elevation. The set was, therefore, virtually useless for directing 'unseen' fire.

Had times been normal the gunners would have withheld their fire rather than waste expensive shells, but these were not normal times. There was strong political pressure on General Frederick Pile, the Commander of Anti-Aircraft Command, to present the sounds of an effective anti-aircraft defence even if the shells burst nowhere near the night raiders. The civilian population, ensconced in their shelters, would never know the difference. Accordingly Pile ordered his gunners to maintain a steady fire when night raiders were over the capital even if there was no accurate fire control information. Later he wrote:

'The volume of fire which resulted, and which was publicized as a "barrage," was in fact largely wild and uncontrolled shooting. There were, however, two valuable results from it: the volume of fire had a deterrent effect upon at least some of the German aircrews . . . there was also a marked improvement in civilian morale.'

During September the gunners had loosed off about a quarter of a million anti-aircraft shells at night, most of them into thin air, and shot down less than a dozen enemy planes.

Ground crewmen turning the crank handle for the inertia starter of a Junkers 88, and one of these aircraft taxi-ing out, for a night attack on Britain.

At this time the fighters the RAF operated at night were no more effective than the guns. The Blenheim had the endurance to mount long patrols and some carried an early type of airborne interception (AI) radar; but the type had little margin of performance over the enemy bombers, so even if it found them it could rarely catch them. The single-seat Spitfires and Hurricanes sent to patrol at night had the performance to catch any raiders they found, but their endurance was short and since they lacked radar they could rarely find the enemy. The Defiant had a short endurance and no radar; but with two pairs of eyes to search for the enemy and the performance to catch them, and the gun turret to enable surprise attacks to be made from below and one side of the target, it was the most effective night fighter available in any numbers.

The twin-engined Beaufighter seemed to provide an effective answer to the night raider. It had a good endurance, it was heavily armed, it had an excellent performance and it was fitted with the latest type of AI radar. The new fighter was being pushed into service as quickly as possible, but it was suffering from teething troubles and some months would elapse before it was operational in sufficient numbers to pose a serious threat to the night raiders.

During their night attacks the German bomber crews were often guided to targets by *Knickebein* radio beams from powerful ground transmitters situated in France, Holland, Germany and Norway. Flying along a beam aligned on his target, a pilot heard morse dots if he was to the left of the beam, morse dashes if he was to the right of the beam and a steady note if he was in the centre of the beam and therefore on track for the target. A second *Knickebein* beam crossed the first at the bomb release point, and the bombs could be released with reasonable accuracy even if the crew could not see the target.

By the end of August the Luftwaffe had twelve *Knickebein* transmitters positioned to align their beams on targets in Britain. But also by then RAF Intelligence had learned about the system and a specialized jamming unit, No 80 Wing, was formed to radiate jamming signals on the German beam frequencies. During the heavy night raids on Britain in September and

The Myth of the London Gun 'Barrage'

Professor Sir Archibald Hill, Air Defence Research Committee

'One cubic mile of space contains 5,500,000,000 cubic yards. The lethal zone of a 3.7in shell is only a few thousand cubic yards and exists for only about 1/50th of a second. The idea of a ''barrage'' of anti-aircraft shells is nonsense. The word ought to be dropped; it gives a false impression, and is based on sloppy thinking and bad arithmetic. Nothing but aimed fire is of any use. In order to give a one-fiftieth chance of bringing down an enemy plane moving at 250 miles per hour and crossing a vertical rectangle ten miles wide and four miles high (from the barrage balloons to 25,000 feet) about three thousand 3.7in shells would be required a second.'

Fighter-Bomber Tactics over London

Oberleutnant Viktor Kraft, Me 109 fighter-bomber pilot, Lehrgeschwader 2

'During the attacks on London we approached the city at about 8,000 metres [26,000 feet], with our own fighter escort. At such altitudes the Me 109 was not easy to fly when carrying a bomb. Usually we flew in an open three-aircraft Vic formation, and closed up to within 20 metres before bombing.

'As we approached the target we would descend to 6,000 metres [19,500 feet] and the leader would bank his aircraft steeply on its side, to pick out the target and line up on it. Against a large target like London we would release our bombs in horizontal flight, letting go when we saw the leader release his.'

◀ A battery of 3.7in anti-aircraft guns firing a salvo from a position in Hyde Park. Despite the wartime propaganda on the effectiveness of the London gun defences, the uncontrolled shooting caused little damage to enemy aircraft and did not cause undue worry to their crews. The guns were however successful in forcing most of the raiders to attack from altitudes above 16,000ft, with a consequent reduction in bombing accuracy. And for those living in the capital the noise of the guns firing and shells exploding provided the shadow, if not the substance, of an effective air defence. (Central Press)

October, No 80 Wing's jamming caused many a German bomber to miss the target. Given the ineffectiveness of the other systems, the Wing formed a significant part of the nation's air defences.

Throughout October, apart from a few nuisance raids by individual bombers, the great majority of the daylight attacks on Britain were carried out by bomb-carrying Messerschmitt 109s and 110s. The fighter-bombers carried small bomb loads – a maximum of 550 pounds for an Me 109 and 2,200 pounds for an Me 110. Moreover during the attacks on London and other large targets the fighter-bombers bombed from high altitude. Since the

aircraft were not fitted with proper bomb-sights, their bombing accuracy was poor. Compared with the concentrated damage caused previously by twin-engined bombers attacking by day, or the widespread destruction being caused by the night bombers, the damage inflicted by the fighter-bombers was insignificant.

Politically it was unacceptable to allow enemy planes to attack London at will, and Fighter Command had to make every effort to engage these fleeting targets. As the Luftwaffe intended, the fighter-bomber raids presented an extremely difficult interception problem. Running in at altitudes around 25,000 feet or

The *Knickebein* beam in fact comprised two overlapping beams, with morse dots radiated in one and morse dashes in the other; where the beams overlapped the dots and the dashes interlocked to produce a steady note. The bomber crew flew along the steady note lane from one transmitter, and released their bombs as they passed through the steady note lane from a second transmitter which crossed the first at the bomb release point. Using transmitters situated in France, Holland, Germany and Norway, the Luftwaffe could align two or more beams over any target in Britain. Using this system, raiders could release their bombs with sufficient accuracy to hit a large area such as a city without having to see the target.
▼

▶ *Knickebein* beam transmitter at Mount Pincon in Normandy, used to guide night bombers to targets in Britain.

A: Approach beam.
B: Cross beam.
C: Bomb release point.

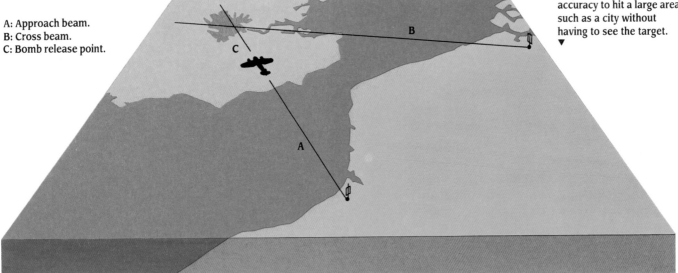

On the evening of 14 October a bomb fell in Balham High Street about 100 yards from the underground station, and blew out a large crater that took the top off the Northern Line tunnel and caused severe flooding. The bomb exploded about 25 yards in front of the moving bus and driver George Hitchen had a narrow escape; he was blown from his cab and ended up in a shop doorway with cuts and bruises. Others were less fortunate. Sixty-eight people were killed in the incident, many of whom had been taking shelter in the station. It was more than three months before the damage was repaired and the line reopened.

above, the bomb-carrying Messerschmitts could reach the outskirts of the capital within 17 minutes of the first radar warning of their approach. From the scramble order, a squadron of Spitfires required about 22 minutes to reach 25,000 feet (a squadron of Hurricanes required about three minutes longer). Thus, if they were to engage the enemy raiders before they reached London, the defending fighters needed to be airborne and at 10,000 feet or above when the first radar plots were received on the incoming fighter-bombers.

To meet the new threat No 11 Group was forced to mount standing patrols over south-eastern England. It meant a lot of flying and general wear and tear on the Spitfires and Hurricanes, for relatively little action, but there was no alternative. Fighters were sent off in relays to cruise on set patrol lines at 15,000 feet, the highest altitude at which they could operate without their pilots needing to use the limited supply of oxygen. When an incoming raiding force was detected on radar, the fighters climbed to altitude and were vectored into position to engage the intruders.

Representative of the actions during this period were those fought between dawn on 15 October and dawn on the 16th. During the morning of the 15th two separate formations

Hell on Earth – 1

Peter Elstob, Notting Hill, London

'One evening after the sirens had sounded their usual warning and nothing had happened, there was a sound like stones being thrown against the house or a number of slates falling off the roof. We ran to the front door and found an incendiary bomb burning brightly on the mat. Roland dashed upstairs for a bucket of sand he kept for just such an emergency; I ran to the kitchen and snatched up a bowl of washing-up water. The suds doused the bomb, snuffing it like a candle.

'From the doorway we could see that there were many other incendiaries, some burning out harmlessly in the road or basement areas, some on houses, and one on the back seat of a car, having burned through the roof. Roland dumped his bucket of sand on that one and was pleased that it obediently went out. The bombs were about nine inches long and burned with a white light for three or four minutes, leaving only their tail fins . . .

'The daughter of a trapped woman was standing on her doorstep crying hysterically. Roland asked her which room her mother was in. "Second floor, back, but she's dead. Oh, poor mum, she's dead, I know she's dead."

'Roland gave me a full bucket of water and kept the stirrup pump himself. We soaked handkerchiefs, tied them over our nose and mouth and went up the smoke-filled stairs on our hands and knees. He kicked open the bedroom door. The room was full of smoke but there was a red glow in one corner and he crawled towards this. I pumped and he directed the spray.

'The incendiary had crashed through the roof and the bedroom ceiling, landing on the bed. All the smoke in the house was coming from the burning mattress and bedding. The bomb had long since burned itself out and the spray soon had the fire out. As the smoke cleared we could see an old lady in the bed. She was quite dead.

'Once outside again we were grabbed by a little old man in a white muffler who begged us to put out some incendiaries lodged in his attic. We got these out fairly quickly but he then pointed to a ladder and an open sky-light, saying that there were more on the roof. Somehow I found myself edging along the peak of the roof clutching a stirrup pump while Roland came behind with a bucket.

From up there we could see down into the street and away over the rooftops. It was an extraordinary sight: all around the horizon fires glowed, searchlights slowly raked the dark sky, anti-aircraft guns flashed silently, there being no apparent connection between them and the almost continuous noise of the guns. High above us shells burst like fireworks. But the most insistent noise came from the street immediately beneath us. It was the excited sound of many people shouting as they scurried in and out of their houses.

'I started to spray the incendiary lodged by the chimney when I heard the sound of more bombs coming down and hugged the peak of the roof. Moments later a stick of small, 50-pound high explosive bombs fell in a line across houses and street.

'The bombers, earlier in the evening, had dropped nothing but hundreds of incendiaries. But this wave, a couple of hours later, came back with instantaneous high-explosive bombs where the fires were brightest and most people were in the streets.

'The explosions caused panic; people ran back into burning houses or threw themselves into basement areas. I heard screams above the explosions as I tried to dig myself into the slates of the roof.

'The rain of bombs lasted only a few minutes but it was dawn before the fires were all out and the injured had been taken away. We sat in the kitchen of our house drinking cocoa with neighbours who had lived near each other for years but had never spoken. Now they were talking and gesticulating in a most un-English manner as they described the narrow escapes of the night.'

DEFIANT VICTORY

OVER BRENTWOOD, 1.55 AM, 16 OCTOBER. On patrol to the east of London in his Defiant, Pilot Officer Desmond Hughes of No 264 Squadron suddenly realized that his aircraft was not alone:

'It was a bright moonlight night. Suddenly, out of the corner of my eye I saw something move across the stars out to my left. If you are scanning the night sky it is normally completely still, so anything that moves attracts the eye. This just had to be another aircraft. I got Fred [Sgt Fred Gash, the gunner] to swing his turret round and we both kept an eye on the black shape. We moved towards it and soon caught sight of a row of exhausts. It was a twin-engined aircraft. I slid alongside, below and to the right of him, and slowly edged in "under his armpit" while Fred kept his guns trained on the aircraft. Then we saw the distinctive wing and tail shape of a Heinkel – there was no mistaking it. I moved into a firing position, within about 50 yards of his wing tip and slightly below, so that Fred could align his guns for an upward shot at about 20 degrees. Obviously the German crew had not seen us, they continued straight ahead.

'Fred fired straight into the starboard engine. One round in six was a tracer, but what told us we were hitting the Heinkel was the glitter of the de Wilde [incendiary] rounds as they ignited on impact. Fred fired, realigned, fired again. He got off two or three bursts. There was no return fire from the bomber – indeed, I doubt if any guns could have been brought to bear on our position on its beam. The engine burst into flames, then the Heinkel rolled on its back, went down steeply and crashed into a field near Brentwood. We heard later that two of the crew baled out and were taken prisoner.'

▲ Defiant of No 264 Squadron taxies out for a night interception patrol. (IWM)

▼ Dornier 17 of BG 3 with dark-painted undersides worn by night bombers operating over England in the autumn of 1940: (Schultz)

of Messerschmitts fought their way through to London and dropped their bombs over a large area. The only significant damage was to Waterloo station, which was hit by a bomb that halted services for several hours until repairs could be effected. Also during the day German fighters flew sweeps over southern England. In a series of scrappy actions seven Messerschmitt 109 fighters and fighter-bombers were shot down, but the RAF lost twelve aircraft.

After dark on the 15th the Luftwaffe delivered yet another heavy attack on London, starting at 8.40 pm and continuing through to 4.40 am the following morning. It was a bright moonlight night and the raiding force of some 400 bombers approached the city at altitudes above 16,000 feet. The vanguard of the raiding

▲
The Bristol Beaufighter, the first really effective night fighter to enter service with the RAF, became available in useful numbers towards the end of 1940. Its maximum speed was 312mph and it was armed with four 20mm cannon and six 0.303in machine-guns.

◄
From the beginning of October almost all daylight attacks on England were carried out by fighter-bombers. Here a Messerschmitt 109 of FG 26 is seen fitted with a 550lb bomb, about to take off for a sortie. (Schoepfel)

◄
Hurricane flown by Pilot Officer Trevor Parsons of No 504 Squadron, at readiness at Filton near Bristol in September 1940. (No 504 Sqn Association)

force, drawn from Air Fleet 2, came in from the direction of Holland. Succeeding aircraft came in from Holland and Belgium over the Thames estuary, and from various points in northern France crossing the south coast of England between Bognor and Dungeness. The German crews reported barrage fire over the capital, with shells detonating at altitudes between 13,000 and 20,000 feet, strongest over the eastern and southern sectors.

One of the pilots taking part in the raid was Guenther Unger of Bomber Geschwader 76, recently promoted to Feldwebel. His crew was one of several that flew two sorties that night, one on the evening of the 15th and another on the morning of the 16th. On both occasions his target was in the dock area and his orders were to remain over the target for as long as possible, to circle overhead and release one bomb every five minutes or so to cause maximum disruption to those on the ground. Displaying a realistic contempt for the so-called 'barrage', Unger spent about twenty-five minutes circling over the target on each sortie.

Forty-one RAF fighters took off to engage the night raiders, but there were only two interceptions. One was by a Blenheim of No 23 Squadron, whose radar operator made contact with one of the enemy bombers. The plane's poor performance prevented it getting into a firing position, however, and after a long tail-chase the raider escaped. The other interception, by Pilot Officer Hughes and Sergeant Gash in a Defiant of No 264 Squadron, resulted in the destruction of a Heinkel 111 of Bomber Gruppe 126 that crashed near Brentwood. The engagement, probably the defenders' only success during the hours of darkness, is described in more detail elsewhere in this book.

That night London's rail system was hit particularly hard. The termini at St Pancras, Marylebone, Broad Street, Waterloo and Victoria were all put out of action for varying periods. Further damage reduced traffic into and out of Euston, Cannon Street, Charing Cross and London Bridge stations. A chance hit blew a large hole in the Fleet sewer, allowing the waters to escape and flood the rail tunnel between Farringdon Street and King's Cross stations. Beckton gas works, Battersea Power Station and the BBC headquarters at

Hell on Earth – 2

Mrs E. M., Carshalton

'They had said there was a risk from incendiary bombs and the safest place to sleep was on the ground floor. So we moved two single beds down for my two eldest sons. I slept upstairs on my own, as my husband was away on duty with an ARP heavy rescue team. We had all gone to bed, the four youngest children in the shelter in the garden.

'This oil bomb hit the house about 3 o'clock in the morning. I never heard a thing. Then a high-explosive bomb landed nearby and that woke me up, it threw me out of bed and on to the landing. When I got downstairs the whole room was on fire. There was dreadful black oil all over the place, burning. My 18-year-old son was trapped in his bed. He couldn't move, his legs must have been damaged when the bomb came through the ceiling. He was alight from head to foot, sitting up in bed. My other son who had been sleeping in the room, my next-door neighbour and I tried to pull him away from the bed, but his skin came away in our hands. He didn't scream or anything, he was just shaking his head from side to side. All he said to me was "Save yourself!" We threw a bucket of water over him, but water was no good against oil. So we threw a bucket of sand over him and that put out some of the flames.

'Then an ambulance came and they carted us away to hospital. I was moaning the whole time and I heard the nurse say, "Admit her, admit her!" I had broken my ankle and my arms and hands were burned. I was wearing a nightdress and a coat, they had to cut them off me. I was so ill with shock that I had several blankets and a couple of hot water bottles and I was still shivering.

'I never saw my eldest son again. He died the next morning, they said from shock. I was in hospital for a week then I discharged myself. My 16-year-old son was also burned, he was in hospital for three weeks then he came out on crutches. The children in the shelter were all right. I wanted to go home, but I had no home. The house was burned down and I had lost all my furniture. So we went to my brother-in-law's.

'Ever since then I have been terrified of fire. It just creeps up on you, you don't hear anything.'

The Fate of One of Those Bombed Out

Mass Observation survey

'I slept the night in the cinema. It is lit by six large lights; four of these are turned off at eleven o'clock, the other two remain on all night. Firemen and nurses patrol the cinema throughout the night, the nurses tucking up children, fetching water and milk, and so on. Each family takes a small piece of ground as their own province. Some are in the orchestra pit, and are given a little privacy by the curtains in front of it. But the majority sleep in the gangways and between the seats. There are about 800 in all in the cinema. All are provided with blankets and palliasses. These they park somewhere and put their belongings (mostly a change of clothing) on the seats nearby. When it is bedtime the men take off their coats, the women their overalls, and lie down. The gangways become crowded, people lying very close to one another. Between the seats there is perhaps an average of one person to a row of ten seats. Here and there is a baby in his pram. There is no noise during the night, except of babies crying. Nearly every mother has a small child, and as soon as one cries, three or four others start too. It is quite impossible to get more than ten minutes' uninterrupted sleep.'

As summer turned to autumn a greater proportion of missions were flown at night and in poor weather, and both sides lost numerous aircraft in flying accidents.
◄
Hurricane of No 504 Squadron, tipped on its nose after running into soft ground at Filton in October. (Mrs T. Tutt)
►
This Heinkel 111 made a successful belly landing on a beach on the French Biscay coast, but was wrecked by the sea when the tide came in. (Trenkle)

Portland Place were hit, three large water mains were fractured and there was wide-spread damage in residential areas. More than 900 fires were reported in the capital, six of which were 'major' and nine 'serious.'

Although London was the bombers' main target on the night of 15th/16th, it was not the only one. Twenty Heinkels of Bomber Gruppe 100 attacked Birmingham, eight Dorniers of Bomber Gruppe 606 raided Bristol. Elsewhere bombs fell on Southend, Windsor, Portsmouth and Yeovil, Southampton, Bournemouth, Plymouth, Tunbridge Wells, Hastings, Reigate and Eastbourne.

The day and night actions over Britain continued in this vein throughout October, punctuated by periods of autumnal bad weather that restricted air activity on twelve days that month. On the night of 6th/7th the weather over the German bases was so bad that even the attack on London had to be cancelled, allowing the capital's citizens a rare respite from their nightly ordeal.

On the night of 25 October the Italian Air Force made its first appearance over Britain, when it sent sixteen Fiat BR.20 bombers to attack Harwich. None of the Italian bombers was lost to enemy action, but the changeable weather conditions over northern Europe presented the newcomers with a more serious problem. One bomber crashed on take-off, two more ran short of fuel on their return flights and their crews baled out.

Four days later Italian aircraft were over England again, this time by day. On the 29th a force of fifteen Fiat BR.20s, escorted by 73 Fiat CR.42 fighters, carried out a snap attack on Ramsgate. The raiders were not intercepted by defending fighters, but several of the bombers suffered damage from anti-aircraft fire.

Several accounts imply that the daylight part of the Battle of Britain ended on 31st October, but in fact the fighting continued with diminishing intensity well into November. If any action can be said to characterize this running-down phase, it is that of the morning of 1 November. Shortly after daybreak, at 7.35 am, the Hurricanes of Nos 253 and 605 Squadrons took off to mount a standing patrol in the Maidstone area; soon afterwards Spitfires of Nos 41 and 603 Squadrons left the ground for a similar patrol over Rochford. Just before 8 am an incoming enemy force was observed on radar leaving the coast of France near Boulogne. The strength of the hostile force was assessed as '9 plus'. At 8.05 am about ten high-flying Messerschmitt 109 fighter-bombers, with fighter escort, crossed the coast near Dover. The raiders penetrated to the Sittingbourne area, dropped their bombs and made off before they could be intercepted.

Fifteen minutes later a similar formation of fighter-bombers with escorts crossed the coast heading for Canterbury. The eleven Hurricanes of No 605 Squadron intercepted the Messerschmitts near Faversham and a sharp combat developed. The sole loss on either side was the Hurricane commander, Squadron Leader Archie McKellar, who was shot down and killed. No 253 Squadron attempted to join in the engagement, but by the time it arrived the last of the Messerschmitts were disappearing in the distance. Neither Spitfire squadron made contact with the enemy.

For a while there was a period of calm, and fresh squadrons took off and moved into

NIGHT BLITZ AND TIP AND RUN – AIRCRAFT LOSSES

Note: On each night during this period, with the exception of that of 6 October when poor weather prevented operations, there was a large-scale attack on London. On some nights other cities were attacked also.

	Luftwaffe	RAF	Main Daylight Action
1 October	5	6	Fighter-bomber attacks on SE England
2 October	15	1	Fighter sweeps over S England
3 October	7	1	Poor weather, little activity
4 October	12	1	Poor weather, little activity
5 October	12	5	Fighter-bomber attack on London
6 October	5	2	Poor weather, little activity
7 October	20	15	Attack on Yeovil
8 October	12	3	Fighter-bomber attack on London
9 October	8	2	Fighter-bomber attack on London
10 October	5	6	Fighter-bomber attack on London
11 October	7	9	Fighter-bomber attacks on SE England
12 October	12	9	Fighter-bomber attacks on SE England
13 October	4	2	Fighter-bomber attacks on SE England
14 October	3	1	Little activity
15 October	8	12	Fighter-bomber attack on London
16 October	12	1	Poor weather, little activity
17 October	11	4	Fighter-bomber attack on London
18 October	14	4	Poor weather, little activity
19 October	2	0	Poor weather, little activity
20 October	12	5	Fighter-bomber attack on London
21 October	5	0	Poor weather, little activity
22 October	10	6	Poor weather, little activity
23 October	4	0	Poor weather, little activity
24 October	6	1	Poor weather, little activity
25 October	20	12	Fighter-bomber attacks on SE England
26 October	10	6	Fighter-bomber attacks on SE England
27 October	14	12	Fighter-bomber attacks on SE England
28 October	7	1	Attacks on shipping
29 October	22	9	Fighter-bombers attacked London, Italian aircraft attacked Ramsgate
30 October	7	7	Poor weather, little activity
31 October	2	0	Poor weather, little activity
1 November	4	9	Fighter-bomber attacks on SE England. Attack on shipping
TOTALS	297	152	

position on the patrol lines. At 10.15 am four Spitfires of No 92 Squadron were directed to intercept a single high-flying intruder over Kent. Five minutes later the defenders sighted the enemy plane at 29,000 feet near Dover, a Messerschmitt 110 on reconnaissance. Two Spitfires reached firing positions and their pilots reported hits; when last seen the plane was heading out to sea streaming glycol from its damaged cooling system. The Messerschmitt crash-landed near Calais with both crewmen wounded.

At 11 am Hurricanes of Nos 229 and 615 Squadrons were on patrol over Maidstone when the next raiding force, about 35 Messerschmitt 109s in two formations, crossed the coast near Dover. Hurricanes of Nos 253 and 501 Squadrons were immediately scrambled to reinforce the defence, and all four squadrons were vectored towards the raiders. None of the Hurricanes made contact however.

Half an hour later Spitfires of Nos 74 and 92 Squadrons, then on the Maidstone patrol line, had a brush with Messerschmitts but there were no losses on either side.

So ended the action on the morning of 1 November. For the pilots of Fighter Command it was a frustrating period, with much time spent waiting on the patrol lines or at readiness on the ground and few chances to engage the enemy.

During the period between 1 October and 1 November, the Luftwaffe lost 297 aircraft while the RAF lost 152 fighters. That meant a ratio of 1.9:1 in favour of the defenders, higher than during the previous phase although set against a background of far less intensive fighting.

Just as the Battle of Britain had begun with a gradual build-up over several weeks in July and the early part of August, the daylight actions over southern England ran down gradually throughout October and November. The night raids on Britain's cities would continue with undiminished fervour throughout the winter and into the spring 1941, ending with a crescendo in May before the main part of the German bomber force moved to bases in the east in preparation for the invasion of the Soviet Union. Only after Hitler had committed his war machine to that all-consuming adventure would the British people gain a lasting respite from the devastating air attacks.

5. THE BATTLE OF BRITAIN SUMMED UP

'A victory is very essential to England at the moment.'
Admiral Sir John Jervis after the battle of Cape St Vincent, 1797

ADOLF HITLER CONCEDED DEFEAT in the Battle of Britain when, on 17 September, he ordered that the planned invasion of southern England be postponed until further notice. During the weeks that followed the ships and barges concentrated at the Channel ports gradually dispersed, never to return.

During the Second World War three major battles signalled the end of the initial, defensive, phase of the conflict for the Allies: in the west, the Battle of Britain; in Russia, the halting of the German advance in front of Moscow; and in the Pacific, the Battle of Midway. In each case, following a succession of disastrous military setbacks, Allied forces secured a victory that stopped the Axis advance in its tracks and established a breathing space in which to build up their strength before going over to the offensive. The Battle of Britain was the first of those decisive battles and, arguably, the most important: had it not been won by the Royal Air Force, the other battles might never have taken place; or, if they had taken place, their outcome might have been different. That is the historical significance of the air battle fought over the south of England during the summer and autumn of 1940.

ALTHOUGH SOME OF THE FIGHTING took place before that time and some occurred after it, the major actions of the Battle of Britain took place between 10 July and 1 November 1940. During

High jinks among the Squadron's sergeant pilots, with H. Jones on the left and 'Wag' Haw on the right. (via Tongue)

With the coming of autumn the air fighting tapered off, giving time to relax after the previous weeks' exertions. These scenes were taken at No 504 Squadron then based at Filton.

▶ **'Suzie', the Squadron's mascot. (504 Sqn Association)**

◀ **Pilot Officers Trevor Parsons (left) and Tony Rook waiting at readiness. (via Tongue)**

The part played by ULTRA during the Battle of Britain

Since the revelation in recent years of the success of the British Ultra cipher-breaking operation at Bletchley Park, some accounts have implied that information from this source governed the tactical handling of Fighter Command during the Battle of Britain. In spite of a careful search of the archives and close questioning of those interviewed, the author has found no hard evidence to support that view. Certainly Ultra provided much useful intelligence on the Luftwaffe during the summer of 1940, but the information was usually fragmentary and only rarely was it of immediate use to C-in-C Fighter Command. During the Battle of Britain most Luftwaffe signals were sent by landline and this traffic could not be picked up in England. Comparatively little traffic relating to the Battle was passed by wireless, and only a small proportion of that was decrypted and read by British Intelligence.

Often the information received via Ultra was too vague to be of operational value. For example, between 9 and 13 August several decrypted signals referred to 'Adlertag' ('Eagle Day'). But neither the code-breakers at Bletchley Park nor Air Intelligence could discover the exact meaning of the code-name, although obviously it referred to a major operation in the offing. Only after the operation had been launched was it clear that 'Adlertag' referred to the first day of a large-scale attack on airfields and other targets in the south of England.

There were other limitations on the value of Ultra information that prevented Air Chief Marshal Dowding from relying on this source when deploying his forces to meet attacks. Although the code-breakers sometimes provided advance notice of the timing and the forces committed to individual raids, in such signals the Germans referred to targets by their serial number in the Luftwaffe target catalogue; for example, Kenley airfield was Target No 10118, Northolt airfield was Target No 10160. The meaning of individual target numbers would become known to RAF Intelligence only over a long period, and throughout the Battle of Britain the meanings of most of them were unknown.

Also the Luftwaffe made frequent last-minute alterations of its attack plans to take into account the weather and other factors, and often these changes were not picked up at Bletchley Park. For example, on 14 September de-crypts revealed that a large-scale attack was to take place against London that day, and they listed the forces that would take part. But previous de-crypts had announced that the raid was scheduled for late on the afternoon of 13 September and it did not take place. In the event the raid was launched on the morning of 15 September, with no further warning from Ultra.

During the Battle of Britain, the first reliable indication of the approach of raiding forces came when those forces appeared on radar. And it was on this information, and not that from Ultra, that the defending fighters were deployed.

Clearly the Luftwaffe had lost the Battle of Britain, for it gained none of the objectives it set out to achieve. But, it is pertinent to ask, could the Germans ever have won the Battle? Throughout the Battle of Britain a primary aim of the Luftwaffe was the destruction of RAF Fighter Command as an effective fighting force. There were four methods available to the Luftwaffe for achieving this: by the destruction of fighters in the air; by the destruction of fighter airfields and fighters on the ground; by the destruction of the fighter control system, including the radar stations; and by the destruction of factories producing fighters.

The German tactics of sending escorted formations of bombers to attack targets in southern England were successful in forcing the RAF fighter squadrons to do battle; but in the combats that followed, the German fighter force was unable to inflict decisively heavy losses on the defenders.

Nor did the attacks on airfields weaken Fighter Command to any significant extent. All No 11 Group's main sector stations, at Tangmere, Kenley, Biggin Hill, Hornchurch and North Weald, were hit hard but none was put out of action for more than a few hours. With the general-purpose bombs available to the Luftwaffe, it was almost impossible to crater a grass airfield so severely that no clear strip 700 yards long remained from which fighters could operate. In any case, craters could quickly be filled with rubble and rolled flat and each station had an efficient organization to do that. Only one Fighter Command airfield was put out of action for any length of time and that one, Manston, was not a sector station. The attacks on airfields failed to destroy fighters on the ground in significant numbers – squadrons at readiness were usually airborne and clear of their base long before an attack developed. Between 13 August and 6 September airfields in southern England were attacked on almost every day, but less than a score of fighters were destroyed on the ground.

Some commentators have suggested that had the Luftwaffe continued its attack on the radar stations along the south coast of England, these vital installations could have been knocked out and Fighter Command deprived of the early warning necessary for its

that period the Luftwaffe lost 1,598 aircraft destroyed or damaged beyond repair in combat, and the RAF lost 902 fighters. The overall ratio of losses throughout the Battle was 1.8:1 in favour of the defenders.

squadrons to go into action effectively. But the radar stations were small pinpoint targets and, as we have seen, they were extremely difficult to hit from the air. Damage to the radar stations could usually be repaired quickly, and where it could not, Fighter Command possessed mobile reserve equipments that could rapidly be moved into place to plug the gaps in the radar cover. Although several radar stations were attacked and damaged, only one (at Ventnor) remained out of action for more than a few hours.

Finally, as a means of reducing the effectiveness of Fighter Command, the Luftwaffe could attack the factories producing the fighter airframes and engines. Spitfire production was centred at Woolston, Itchen and Eastleigh near Southampton, with production building up at the new plant at Castle Bromwich near Birmingham. Hurricanes were produced at Langley in Buckinghamshire, Brooklands and Kingston in Surrey, and at Brockworth in Gloucestershire. The Merlin engines that powered these fighters were built at the Rolls-Royce plants at Derby, Crewe and Glasgow. Scores of factories throughout the country acted as sub-contractors, producing components for these fighters and their engines.

The Luftwaffe could certainly have done more to attack the factories producing fighters, especially those around Southampton and in Surrey that could be reached by escorted bomber formations. Yet, as we have seen, when the factories at Woolston and Itchen were bombed successfully, it took only a few weeks to disperse the production of Spitfires into the surrounding area and resume it there. Once they were dispersed in this way, aircraft production facilities were almost invulnerable to air attack. Later in the war RAF Bomber Command and the US Army Air Forces, with far larger and more effective fleets of bombers, mounted a massive and sustained attack on the German aircraft industry lasting more than a year, but failed to cause any major drop in production. With the much smaller resources at its command, the Luftwaffe could not have done any better.

At no time did the combined attack on Fighter Command seriously weaken it. Throughout the Battle the Command possessed an average of fifty squadrons with a

---

A Squadron Commander Remembers

Squadron Leader Michael Crossley, No 32 Squadron

'Other squadrons piled up bigger scores (even if they did take longer to do it), other squadrons have received more publicity. Everyone thinks (or ought to think) that his is "The Best Squadron in the Air Force", but I guarantee there was no happier squadron in the Air Force than 32. I consider it the greatest privilege of my life to have served with such a magnificent bunch of boys who have proved themselves to be as good as they thought they were, and who had enhanced the reputation that the Squadron earned in the last war.

'I loved that Squadron better than anything in the world. I know that when I got the signal one evening to say that I was posted and it slowly dawned on me that after 4½ of the happiest years I was actually going to leave 32, I strolled out on to the aerodrome and cried like a baby. I simply couldn't help it. Funny. It gets you that way.'

Pilots of No 32 Squadron (left to right): Pilot Officer R. Smythe, Sergeant J. Proctor, Pilot Officer K. Gilman, Flight Lieutenant Peter Brothers, Pilot Officer D. Grice, Pilot Officer P. Gardner, and Pilot Officer Alan Eckford.

total of just over a thousand fighters; of that thousand, an average of 720 aircraft were available for operations on any one day. Although there were shortfalls from time to time, in general the manufacture and repair of fighters kept pace with losses and at the beginning of October Fighter Command was as strong as it had been at the beginning of August.

Much has been said of the losses in pilots suffered by Fighter Command and these were indeed serious. But the Luftwaffe was also suffering serious losses in trained personnel. During the large-scale actions, for each RAF pilot killed or wounded, it cost the Luftwaffe five or more aircrew killed, wounded or taken

British poster commemorating the Battle of Britain and paraphrasing Winston Churchill's famous words to the House of Commons. (Imperial War Museum)

prisoner. The ratio of 5:1 was close to that between the number of German aircrew involved in the Battle, and those in Fighter Command. In other words, the two sides suffered similar losses in trained aircrew, in proportion to their overall strengths. Had it persisted in its attempt to smash Fighter Command, the Luftwaffe would have been as likely to smash itself.

Given the quality of the leadership, the training and the equipment of Fighter Com-mand and the high morale of its personnel, given the ability of the British aircraft industry to build and repair fighters in sufficient numbers, given the resilience of the British people in the face of air attack and, finally – and probably most important of all – given the ability of Winston Churchill to rouse the nation to action, given these factors the Battle of Britain could never have been won by the Luftwaffe. And it does no discredit to 'The Few' to say so.

BIBLIOGRAPHY

Books

Balke, Ulf, *Kampfgeschwader 100*, Motorbuch Verlag, Stuttgart 1981
Barclay, George, *Angels 22*, Arrow Books, London 1971
Barker, E. C., *The Fighter Aces of the R.A.F.*, William Kimber, London 1964
Bekker, Cajus, *The Luftwaffe War Diaries*, Macdonald, London 1964
Bickers, Richard Townsend, *Ginger Lacey, Fighter Pilot*, Robert Hale, London 1962
Bishop, Edward, *Their Finest Hour*, Ballantine, New York 1968
Boorman, H. R. P., *Hell's Corner 1940*, Kent Messenger, Maidstone
Brickhill, Paul, *Reach for the Sky*, Collins, London 1957
Bruetting, Georg, *Das waren die Deutschen Kampflieger Asse 1939-1945*, Motorbuch Verlag, Stuttgart 1975
Carne, Daphne, *The Eyes of the Few*, Macmillan, London 1970
Churchill, Winston, *The Second World War*, Volume 2, Cassell, London 1948

Collier, Basil, *The Defence of the United Kingdom*, HMSO London 1952
Collier, Richard, *Eagle Day*, Hodder and Stoughton, London 1972
Dierich, Wolfgang, *Die Verbände der Luftwaffe 1935-1945* Motorbuch Verlag, Stuttgart 1976
– *Kampfgeschwader 55*, Motorbuch Verlag, Stuttgart 1975
Forrester, Larry, *Fly For Your Life*, Frederick Muller, London 1962
Galland, Adolf, *The First and the Last*, Methuen, London 1955
Green, William, *Warplanes of the Third Reich*, Macdonald and Jane's, London 1970
Grundelach, Karl, *Kampfgeschwader 4*, Motorbuch Verlag, Stuttgart 1978
Hinsley, F. W., *British Intelligence in the Second World War*, HMSO, London, 1979
HMSO Official Publications (authors not named)
– *Front Line, 1940-41. The story of Civil Defence*
– *Roof Over Britain The Story of the AA Defences*
– *The Battle of Britain*
Kiehl, Heinz, *Kampfgeschwader 53*, Motorbuch Verlag, Stuttgart 1983

Mason, Francis, *Battle over Britain*, McWhirter Twins, London 1969
McKee, Alexander, *Strike from the Sky*, Souvenir Press, London 1960
Neil, *Gun Button to Fire*, William Kimber, London 1987
Obermaier, Ernst, *Die Ritterkreuztraeger der Luftwaffe, Jagdflieger 1939-45*, Verlag Diether Hoffman, Mainz 1966
Price, Alfred, *Battle of Britain, The Hardest Day*, Arms and Armour Press, London 1988
– *Blitz on Britain*, Ian Allan, Shepperton 1977
– *Luftwaffe Handbook*, Ian Allan, Shepperton 1986
– *Combat Development in World War Two: Bomber Aircraft*, Arms and Armour Press, London
– *The Spitfire Story*, Arms and Armour Press, London 1986
– *Combat Development in World War Two: Fighter Aircraft*, Arms and Armour Press, London 1989
Ramsey, Winston, et al, *The Battle of Britain, Then And Now*, After the Battle, London 1980
Rawlings, John, *Fighter Squadrons of the R.A.F.*, Macdonald and Jane's, London 1969
Shore, Christopher, and Williams, Clive, *Aces High*, Neville Spearman, London 1966
Wood, Derek, and Dempster, Derek, *The Narrow Margin*, Hutchinson, London 1961
Wright, Robert, *Dowding and the Battle of Britain*, Macdonald and Jane's, London 1972

Magazine Articles

Macmillan, Wing Commander Norman, *Resolving the War's Great Controversy*, Aeronautics magazine, October and November 1960 issues
Marrs, Eric, *152 Squadron: A Personal Diary of the Battle of Britain*, The Aeroplane magazine September 1945

Unpublished Sources

Air Ministry, *Air Defence of the United Kingdom*, copy held in the Public Record Office, Kew
Pilots' Combat Reports, Fighter Command, Group and station records, Anti-Aircraft Command records, Home Office records, held in Public Record Office, Kew
Transcripts of interviews conducted by the author

Equivalent Ranks

Royal Air Force	Luftwaffe	Royal Air Force	Luftwaffe
Marshal of the Royal Air Force	Generalfeld-marschall	Flying Officer	Oberleutnant
		Pilot Officer	Leutnant
		Warrant Officer	Stabsfeldwebel
Air Chief Marshal	Generaloberst	Flight Sergeant	Oberfeldwebel
Air Marshal	General	Sergeant	Feldwebel
Air Vice-Marshal	Generalleutnant	Corporal	Unteroffizier
Air Commodore	Generalmajor	Leading Aircraftman	Obergefreiter
Group Captain	Oberst	Aircraftman First Class	Gefreiter
Wing Commander	Oberstleutnant		
Squadron Leader	Major	Aircraftman Second Class	Flieger
Flight Lieutenant	Hauptmann		